RET~~URN~~

MW00988627

"Jen Thompson uses her authentic voice to weave together a beautiful book full of hope, truth, and love. She reminds us we can return to Him, even when we mess up, even when we feel like we don't belong. His love is never-ending. Hallelujah!"
—LESLIE MEANS, founder of Her View from Home and bestselling author of *So God Made a Mother*

"*Return to Jesus* is an irresistible invitation to rest in the presence of Christ every day. We don't have to wait for heaven to enjoy Jesus; we can enjoy Him right now in every ordinary, beautiful, and difficult moment of life. Jen Thompson draws you into a fresh, abiding relationship with Jesus while helping you develop habits and routines so you can go deeper with Him. A must-read for anyone ready to say yes to Jesus's bold and beautiful invitation to abide."
—JENNIFER DUKES LEE, author of *Growing Slow* and *It's All Under Control*

"Jen Thompson invites us to return to the greatest love we will ever experience in this life, and she does so through the sharing of God's Word and her beautiful testimony of Jesus. She so graciously offers practical steps and reflections to help bring your gaze back to Christ and align your heart with the Truth."
—KELLI BACHARA, licensed professional clinical counselor and writer of *The Unraveling* blog

"Jen Thompson's gentle voice provides a heartfelt road map for rediscovering our relationship with Jesus in every season of life. Through stories and gentle insights, she invites us to find Jesus in stillness, view challenges with grace, and lean on Him as our source of strength, hope, and peace. *Return to Jesus* invites us back to love, forgiveness, and purpose, guiding us to a more meaningful life while deepening our connection with the One who offers us life to the full. Thompson's message will resonate in your heart long after you turn the last page."

—NATASHA SMITH, author of *Can You Just Sit With Me?*

"This beautiful invitation back to Jesus is a balm and comfort for the soul. Jen Thompson's vulnerability in sharing her stories reminds us that despite our failings and troubles, He is calling us to relationship with Him. Thompson guides us to remember that we all have a place at His table—all we have to do is sit down. What a gift."

—AMY BETTERS-MIDTVEDT, speaker and author of
You'll Make It (and They Will Too)

"In *Return to Jesus*, Jen Thompson offers a heartfelt invitation to find Christ in every moment—whether beautiful, stressful, or ordinary. With warmth and wisdom, she reminds us that Jesus is constantly reaching out to us, even in the midst of our daily routines, inviting us to abide with Him. This book is a lifeline for anyone longing to experience deeper peace, joy, and connection with Jesus in the everyday moments of life."

—DARREN WHITEHEAD, senior pastor of Church of the City
in Nashville, Tennessee, and author of *The Digital Fast*

"Jen Thompson's invitation to return to Jesus found me right in the middle of a season of feeling worn thin and burned out. Her vulnerability and practical tips will not only help you to abide in Jesus but will also leave you wanting even more of Him. *Return to Jesus* is a much-needed book for the woman longing to ditch the stress and hustle of this world in exchange for more of Jesus. And Thompson is the encouraging friend you want by your side."

—COURTNEY DEVICH, speaker and author of
Mama's Got Anxiety

"Wise, tender, and deeply healing, *Return to Jesus* offers a gentle invitation for our hearts, souls, and minds to return home to the One who loves us—wholly and completely—without conditions."

—MIKALA ALBERTSON, MD, author of
Everything I Wish I Could Tell You About Midlife

RETURN TO JESUS

RETURN TO JESUS

An Invitation to Abide with Him in Every
Beautiful, Stressful, or Tedious Moment

Jen Thompson

WaterBrook

WaterBrook
An imprint of the Penguin Random House Christian Publishing Group,
a division of Penguin Random House LLC
1745 Broadway, New York, NY 10019
waterbrookmultnomah.com
penguinrandomhouse.com

Scripture quotations, unless otherwise indicated, are taken from the Holy Bible, New International Version®, NIV®. Copyright © 1973, 1978, 1984, 2011 by Biblica Inc.™ Used by permission of Zondervan. All rights reserved worldwide. (www.zondervan .com). The "NIV" and "New International Version" are trademarks registered in the United States Patent and Trademark Office by Biblica Inc.™ Used by permission. All rights reserved. Scripture quotations marked (CEV) are from the Contemporary English Version. Copyright © 1991, 1992, 1995 by American Bible Society. Used by Permission. Scripture quotations marked (ESV) are taken from the ESV® Bible (The Holy Bible, English Standard Version®), copyright © 2001 by Crossway, a publishing ministry of Good News Publishers. Used by permission. All rights reserved. Scripture quotations marked (MSG) are taken from The Message, copyright © 1993, 2002, 2018 by Eugene H. Peterson. Used by permission of NavPress. All rights reserved. Represented by Tyndale House Publishers. Scripture quotations marked (NKJV) are taken from the New King James Version®. Copyright © 1982 by Thomas Nelson. Used by permission. All rights reserved. Scripture quotations marked (NLT) are taken from the Holy Bible, New Living Translation, copyright © 1996, 2004, 2015 by Tyndale House Foundation. Used by permission of Tyndale House Publishers, Carol Stream, Illinois 60188. All rights reserved. Scripture quotations marked (WE) are taken from THE JESUS BOOK – The Bible in Worldwide English. Copyright © 1969, 1971, 1996, 1998 by SOON Educational Publications, Derby, DE65 6BN, UK. Used by permission.

A WaterBrook Trade Paperback Original

Copyright © 2025 by Jen Thompson

Penguin Random House values and supports copyright. Copyright fuels creativity, encourages diverse voices, promotes free speech, and creates a vibrant culture. Thank you for buying an authorized edition of this book and for complying with copyright laws by not reproducing, scanning, or distributing any part of it in any form without permission. You are supporting writers and allowing Penguin Random House to continue to publish books for every reader. Please note that no part of this book may be used or reproduced in any manner for the purpose of training artificial intelligence technologies or systems.

WATERBROOK and colophon are registered trademarks of
Penguin Random House LLC.

LIBRARY OF CONGRESS CATALOGING-IN-PUBLICATION DATA
Names: Thompson, Jen, author.
Title: Return to Jesus: inviting his love into every part of your life/Jen Thompson.
Description: Colorado Springs: WaterBrook, 2025
Identifiers: LCCN 2024043179 | ISBN 9780593601297 (trade paperback) | ISBN 9780593601303 (ebook)
Subjects: LCSH: Women—Religious life—Christianity.
Classification: LCC BV4527 .T477 2025 | DDC 248.8/43—dc23/eng/20241115
LC record available at https://lccn.loc.gov/2024043179

Printed in the United States of America on acid-free paper

1st Printing

BOOK TEAM: Production editor: Jocelyn Kiker • Managing editor: Julia Wallace •
Production manager: Angela McNally

Book design by Virginia Norey
Art: Valerii/stock.adobe.com

For details on special quantity discounts for bulk purchases,
contact specialmarketscms@penguinrandomhouse.com.

The authorized representative in the EU for product safety and compliance is
Penguin Random House Ireland, Morrison Chambers, 32 Nassau Street,
Dublin D02 YH68, Ireland, https://eu-contact.penguin.ie.

For Patrick:

You modeled to me what the love of Christ was when I was at my most unlovable. You have sat by my side and walked with me hand in hand through my darkest moments. Thank you for never giving up on me. Even when the world would say you should have. You are forever my soulmate. You are my home.

For Sophia, Amelia, Nylah, and Patrick:

You have taught me more than you will ever know, and my love for you cannot be adequately expressed with words put to any page. Just know I am always and forever in your corner. Cheering for you. Believing in you. Praying for you. Arms wide open and shoulders available for tears—should you feel you have fallen and ever need a place to land.

For anyone who has felt tired, worn, stretched, lost, confused, angry, unlovable, hurt, or unsure if there is a place for you at the table:

I write these words for you. There is always a place. The invitation is always extended. Jesus is waiting. Whenever you are ready to return.

Contents

THE INVITATION

I love receiving an invitation, especially if that invitation arrives in the mail.

I come from a time long, long ago. A time when digital invitations weren't a thing. Back in those ancient days, when computers were still black and white and the "internet" was a new word that carried a lot of mystery and promise, invitations arrived enclosed in stamped envelopes. To either accept or decline this personal request of my presence, I had to either call the sender or mail an RSVP card. Nowadays, paper invitations usually only arrive for select special occasions like graduations, weddings, bridal showers, or baby showers. But the smile they bring to my face remains.

I love looking at the intimate details—the fonts, the words, the imagery, the ornate wisps and flourishes. These things make the invitation unique and personal. The beauty of it all makes me pause and realize the thought that went into this singular piece of paper.

Don't get me wrong: while paper invites give me all the feels, I still love a digital invitation. Any invitation, really. Because to be invited means someone thought of me. My presence means something to someone. And that feels good.

We all receive invitations regularly. Some arrive printed on fancy paper in the mail. Others land in our inboxes. Some via text. And others are verbal. With each invitation comes an underlying message: we are seen, we matter, and someone out there enjoys our company.

Yet, with all these invitations, there is one single, consistent invitation that exists for everyone. An invitation from One who sees us, One who loves us, One who enjoys our company more than we can possibly comprehend. An invitation from Jesus to meet with Him throughout our days. He knocks at the door of our hearts and asks to steep every facet of our lives in His love—our personal lives, our relationships, and our collective Christian experience.

His request arrives in different ways throughout our day, but, sadly, we are often too busy or distracted to even notice. We don't really accept or decline; we just keep plugging along. Our eyes open, our bodies rise, and we move forward with the day, sliding easily into our habits and our rhythms. Doing all those things we usually do—those dirty dishes in the sink, the laundry piled high, and the emails, SignUpGenius requests, Venmo transfers, texts, and more—without a second glance at His invitation. Our daily demands pile up, leaving us frustrated, overwhelmed, and exhausted.

We miss the chance to be refreshed by His presence, find healing in His words, and find direction for our lives. Instead, we're running the other way. We're searching for significance and meaning in the trivial. One day bleeds into the other, and it all starts to feel the same. We are stuck in the mundane.

Yet somewhere deep in our hearts and souls, we know we were created for so much more. We can feel it. There is more to this life than hurried days, packed schedules, fast food on the road, and the never-ending scroll on our phones.

This *more* we long for waits for us. This *more* we long for—whether we know it or not—is to be present with the Lord. And every day, in every way, Jesus reaches out a hand and invites us to experience His abundant life. His kingdom here on Earth. We need only accept.

Like with all requests, the choice is yours. Will you accept what has been offered and receive His peace, love, joy, and many gifts that are waiting for you? Will you sit with the Almighty, feel His tug on your heart, develop rhythms of return that work for you, and experience the blessings He longs to give?

A Personalized Invitation

The idea of an invitation from Jesus seems so abstract, though, doesn't it? I mean, what does it even look like?

Like a personalized invitation in the mail, I believe His call is different for each of us.

My invitation arrives when I look out the window at the leaves blowing in the wind on a fall morning and remember God created all this beauty. Jesus calls me to Him when I hold a friend who has lost her husband, and I remember that while there are no words I can say to take away her pain, God blesses those who mourn with His comfort. I see the invitation when I snuggle with my children and say prayers at night after a long day. If I really stop and think about it, I see Jesus's beautiful and tender invitation all throughout my day.

An invitation to pause and give thanks.

An invitation to see the good.

An invitation to say a prayer for a stranger.

An invitation to meditate on Scripture.

An invitation to sit beside a loved one in pain.

An invitation to live in the joy and the sorrow.

An invitation to love the unlovable.

An invitation to place my bare feet in the grass and look up at the sky and breathe in the gift of the air and the sun on my face and acknowledge that this day was not promised, but I at least have this moment.

When I accept His invitation to return, these moments with my Creator become the altar I worship on. I return to Him in the grind and praise Him for His peace in the chaos. I return to Him in the pain and praise Him for His comfort. I return to Him with my shame and praise Him for His grace. Through every return to Jesus, I am filled with Him.

My relationship with Jesus is the most profound relationship of love and grace I will ever have the privilege of experiencing. Yet I often settle for so much less than what is available. And I miss Him. I miss the love. The peace. The joy. The grace. The relationships. The unity. The healing. All that is found in Jesus. Always in Jesus.

Friend, your choice to either accept or decline does not affect His love for you, but it does affect your days. Your life. Because waiting on the other end of that invitation to meet with Love Himself are the very best gifts you could ever receive. It is an invitation to experience a bit of heaven on Earth. An invitation for your eternity with Him to begin right now. Because heaven isn't just waiting for you on the other side of your last breath. Jesus invites you to taste the bread and drink the wine and see and feel and behold the miracle of the gifts of eternity here and now. Whenever and however you choose to meet with Him. With whatever rhythms and habits you build into your days.

Rhythms to Return

There are rhythms to my days. I wake up and make my bed. I feed the cats (because this must happen first thing. They would have it no other way). I make lunches for the kids before they head out the door. I drive the kids to school. I start a load of laundry. Then I open the stack of journals and devotions sitting on the kitchen island. My day begins and unfolds as usual. I am a creature of habit, and routine is my friend.

In the mindless patterns of my day, my soul longs for more. I long to be with Jesus. I long to return to Him, no matter the season I'm in—quiet and reserved, busy and stressed, joyful and pleasant, painful and filled with tears, or somewhere in between. I long to walk with Him through it all because He is my rock, my salvation, my love, and so much more. And I want to share with you the rhythms I've set to recognize and accept His invitation to return, and the gifts I've found as I've looked to Him in all things.

I have wrestled with my faith and my doubt, with my shame and the lies that I was unlovable. I have been confused and distressed by the words and actions of friends who love the Lord as I do but see the world so differently. I have confessed, shed tears, sought repentance, and received grace. My heart has been undone by the love of the Lord, and I have seen and experienced this love from Him and through others. I have intentionally set patterns of return to Jesus through it all because He is the only Way, Truth, and Light that can guide me on this tumultuous journey we call life.

Returning to Jesus has changed how I experience my days. He has changed my relationships with others. He has changed the way I interact with the communities where I find myself. For that reason, I've broken this book into three parts: your personal return, relational return, and collective return.

Your personal return covers how you can individually return to Jesus as you press forward in your day with all that it requires of you. Part two covers your relational return—how to invite Jesus into your close and personal relationships to experience repair, connection, and so much more with those you love. Finally, part three details how you can return to Jesus with other people collectively—when you gather on Sundays at church, or at a neighborhood potluck. You'll discover how to invite Him into those places and spaces where you reside with your community.

At the end of each chapter is a prayer, questions for reflection, and the invitation to return. The prayer will give you a place to start when reaching out to God. If you feel led, continue the conversation with Him. He loves to hear from you. The questions offer you a moment to pause and unpack parts of the chapter. Breathe deep and let the Lord guide your thoughts. Finally, the invitations are suggestions to help guide you toward new habits and patterns. They are meant to help you recognize the presence of Jesus in your daily life so that you can meet with Him at any time, day or night, in countless ways. But I know that life is busy and time is a precious commodity. So I've broken down these invitations into three intervals of time: one minute, one hour, and one day. Choose the invitation that works for you right now.

These rhythms of return will help you to make Jesus a part of those habits and routines you already have established. They will point you back to the Lord. As your relationship with Him deepens, your life will be transformed in the most miraculous of ways.

Jesus is waiting for you to turn and face Him. To give it all to Him. To stop running from Him and to start running toward Him. To rest in His presence. To lay it at His feet and trust Him enough to never pick it up again. To give Him the chaos of your days and the all-encompassing pain of your grief. To trust Him with those things you want no one to discover. To believe He can take what is broken and turn it into something more beautiful than you ever could have pictured. To meet you in your neighborhood. Your church. At your dining room table. And while you sit with your knees pressed uncomfortably on the hard floor, folding what feels like an endless pile of laundry.

He is in the mundane and the monotonous.

He is in the miraculous and the glorious.

He is in the moment when you drop to your knees because your world has just stopped.

And He is in all the wonder you will ever behold as you breathe in each of your breaths.

He is with your enemy.

And He is with your closest companion.

Friend, I have lived in the valley made of sand, I have climbed to the mountaintop with all its splendor, and I have traveled gravel roads in the in-between. And in it all, He has been there. Even when I forgot to reach for Him. Even when I didn't acknowledge Him. Even when I tried to run from Him.

He has always been there.

He will always be here.

Waiting. Reaching. Loving.

Inviting us to return.

PART ONE

PERSONAL RETURN

Here's my point: the solution to an overbusy life is not more time. It's to slow down and simplify our lives around what really matters.

—John Mark Comer,
The Ruthless Elimination of Hurry

1

RETURN TO LOVE

The Greatest Gift You've Been Given

If we knew how much He loves us, we would always be ready to face life—both its pleasures and its troubles.

—Brother Lawrence, *The Practice of the Presence of God*

The spring day was beautiful, cloudless, with a gentle breeze that helped take the edge off and keep the beads of sweat from forming on brows. It was perfect for strawberry-picking with friends at a local farm where bright red berries dotted the lush green landscape, begging us to put them in our buckets (and a few in our mouths). Visitors, trying to take advantage of the warm weather, filled the parking lots and overflowed into the grass fields.

Soon, the excitement of finding a ripe berry died down and our children began to cry, "It's hot" and "I'm tired." Their groans were an indication it was time to head back. With full buckets held by red-stained fingers, we headed to the minivan in the overflow parking.

My daughter has always been a strong-willed child, and this day was no exception to her boundary-pushing, limit-testing way of life. We were walking together in a tight group, and my daughter was next to me. Then, she broke free. Just like that.

She went from safely by my side to running in a full sprint dead ahead, and in an instant, she was out of my reach.

She wasn't looking at what was in front of her. She was just running as children often do, with her legs pressing forward and an unawareness unique to childhood. She didn't see the rear lights of a car flash red. I knew what that meant, though—that car would soon be in motion, and my daughter was barreling straight for it.

Fear flooded every inch of my being. I yelled as loud as I knew how, my legs racing toward her, but not quite fast enough. Sweat formed on my brow as I screamed, "Nylah! Nylah! Stop! Stop! Stop!"

She was completely unaware of the danger, so engrossed in what she was doing that she could not hear my voice. Finally, she heard me and stopped—an arm's length away from the vehicle. Nylah turned to face me with an oblivious smile while the car began to back out. My body shook, acutely aware of how close I had come to possibly losing her.

When I caught up to Nylah, I scooped her up and wrapped her little body into mine. Consumed with my love for her, I smelled her hair and felt the softness of her freckled cheeks. As I held her, I was overwhelmed with gratitude for the gift of this sweet, strong-willed child and the way her small frame felt against my own. Feeling her in my arms carried a new weight— it had more meaning than just minutes before. I thanked God for keeping her safe, and in the embrace of tenderness between mother and child, God reached for me.

"Here. See Me. In this moment, I'm here. And I love you."

Warmth flooded my soul. I knew without any doubt that my Creator, my Father, felt the same unreserved tenderness for me. He knew the smell of my hair, the shape of my face, and the creases of my personality.

And just as I could see what Nylah could not, God sees the

direction I'm headed, perceives the dangers I'm blind to, and knows the lies I believe. But like a strong-willed child who thinks they know best, I run. He calls out to me. He offers me the truth of who He is and who I am to Him, but I keep pressing forward in the direction I am headed. I focus on the demands weighing on me—my work, my kids, the bills, the dishes, the laundry, life—and feel a soul-level depletion settle in my bones. I am too engrossed to hear His voice calling to me. When I finally hear Him, stop, and turn, He's right there waiting to scoop me up and place me safely back into the comfort of His arms.

He does not greet me with condemnation, guilt, or the many things I attempt to place on myself as a result of being human in a fallen world. No, when God cries out for me and I return to Him, I am wrapped in love.

When I picked up my daughter and held her, I knew the smell of her freshly washed, strawberry-blond hair. I knew the way her eyes crinkle in the corner when she smiles. I knew the look she gives when she is being mischievous. I knew how her body folded into mine. I knew every inch of her because I had spent nearly every day with her since she came into this world.

God has spent eternity with you on His mind. He knows you more intimately than you know yourself. He longs for you to know the depth of His infinite love because He *is* the embodiment of perfect Love. He is love without condition. There are no strings attached. His love is always there. Always waiting. Always inviting.

No matter how far or how long you run. No matter if you aren't listening. No matter the lies you believe. No matter what your head, your heart, or others may tell you—God is there, waiting to scoop you up in His tender arms. To welcome you home with His loving embrace. An invitation to abide in the fullness of His Presence. An invitation to meet with and settle your whole self into the warmth and security of His love.

Return to Jesus

For a very long time, I struggled to believe God loved me.

I heard the messages at church telling me Jesus died for me. I heard the words spoken in sermons and shared at Bible studies. I was told time and time again that I was infinitely and forever loved by my Father above. I sang songs about Jesus loving me, had conversations about this gift all were offered, and would nod in agreement with friends who said things my head knew to be true.

God loves me. Nod. Nod. Nod.

Jesus died for me. Nod. Nod. Nod.

My head understood the invitation and my words declared the truth of this gift, but my heart couldn't catch up with my head and my words. I couldn't hold those truths, because I was being held ransom by lies: I was too broken. Too damaged. Too far gone. I had spent too long away from Him. God doesn't want *me*.

Have you struggled to believe that God loves you, too?

If you answered yes, my guess is somewhere along the way, you picked up a message that said you are unworthy, you aren't enough, you aren't lovable as you are. Then you took that message and made it your truth. You tucked it deep inside your heart, where it festered and grew. Now anytime something, or someone, tries to tell you otherwise, you nod your head in agreement—but deep down, you still feel undeserving, inadequate, or unredeemable.

If this resonates with your heart and if you struggle to believe you can abide in God's love, as you are, with no strings attached—please hear me when I say you are not alone. Many of us grapple with this lie because of trauma and wounding. And many more feel unloved simply because we live in a culture that is consumed with performance, applauds overachievement and success in all forms, and publicly shames those who have been deemed unworthy.

I have good news, though: you can silence the lies that hold your heart captive.

I found freedom through trusted friends who were willing to sit with me, study the Word, and listen to me talk about how I just couldn't really believe I was loved. They were gentle with me and prayed for me. They didn't grow impatient or tired of the fact that I sometimes sounded like a record stuck on repeat—declaring all the reasons I was unworthy and couldn't let my heart grab hold of this truth. I broke through the falsities with counseling and by traveling to the hard places in my life. I untangled trauma. I healed. With time and patience, I learned more about who God really is and who I really am to Him. And every time I would forget, God would reach down and remind me of the depth of His love.

He reached down when my daughter was just inches away from being struck by a car. "Here. See Me. In this moment, I'm here. And I love you." And this wasn't the first time. Even before I held my daughter close, still shaking from the fear of losing her, the weight of His love had cracked my heart open, threatening to undo me, at the birth of my children.

When my first child was born and placed in my arms, I could sense that there was something so much bigger at play than I had ever grasped before. This screaming bundle of mashed hair, wrinkled skin, and deep-blue eyes had not come into this world offering any reason for me to love her. She wasn't asking how she could help. She wasn't caring for me. She wasn't affirming me or bringing me gifts. On the contrary, she was taking up quite a bit of my time, energy, and resources. But none of that mattered. I loved her. And not just a subtle, surface-level, passing love. I loved this child with a ferocity that echoed through my bones. And just when I thought my heart could not possibly hold more love, we had another child, and I learned that love could expand and stretch and grow. With each experience, a question rose in me: *If I love my own children this much, how much more does my Creator love me?*

This one question started an avalanche in my heart. I had believed I could not be loved simply for who I am, but God showed me that I am loved more deeply than I could possibly comprehend because I was His. Love was no longer about my performance or my worthiness or how put-together I seemed on a given day. It was about God. It was about the perfect love my Heavenly Father has for me. A love He made known through His very own Son—Jesus.

John 3:16 is a verse we see often. It's on billboards off the highway, on handwritten signs, on greeting cards, on the black stripes under a sports player's eyes. And, at times, being yelled on street corners of busy cities. It may feel a bit overused, washed down, and sometimes even abused. But let's not let the commercialism of the verse strip it of its power:

> For God so loved the world that he gave his one and only Son, that whoever believes in him shall not perish but have eternal life.[1]

Not "for God was so upset with us" or "for God so needed to control us." Not "for God so liked us" or "for God so wanted to win us over." No. For God so *loved* us. And not just the good people, or the ones we deem worthy—*the world*. Me, you, all of us. And He loved us so much that He gave us His one and only Son to save us.

My heart was overwhelmed with the thought of losing my child on that grassy field many years ago. That "what if" scenario held a pain that seemed too much to bear. My heart breaks deeply for those I know, and also those I don't, who have experienced the death of a child. Yet our God chose to walk that tragic road. He chose the pain. He chose the unimaginable because He so loved.

When we return to Jesus, we return to that love. Not disapproval, manipulation, or anger, but love. And slowly, gently, and tenderly, God replaces the lies we harbor—you aren't good enough; you aren't worthy; you are too damaged, too broken, too far gone—with the truth of His love.

He gave His life for you. The Maker of all the stars in the infinite galaxies chose you. You are worth dying for.[2]

Friend, God loves you. It's okay if you aren't ready for that truth to sink in yet. God knows your hurts. He knows your heart. He knows the healing that needs to take place before you can fully accept the depth of His love. The beautiful thing is, there isn't a time limit. It isn't an "act now or lose the offer" kind of thing. His offer is forever, and He will wait as long as it takes.

The Presence of Love

Whether you aren't quite sure about the whole Jesus thing, believe with your head but aren't quite there with your heart, or are completely arrested by the love of the Lord, you can practice rhythms of returning to His love.

When you are feeling unlovable, I pray that lie is replaced with this truth: you are loved. This love is not based on your life circumstance. Your status. Your gifts. Your weaknesses. What you can accomplish in a day. It has nothing to do with how manicured your lawn may be or how well-behaved your kids are during the Sunday service. This love cannot be earned. It cannot be taken away. When you are feeling unlovable, repeat this truth: "I am a child of the Creator of the Universe. I am made for this time and this space for a reason. I am pursued. I am loved."[3]

Say it as many times as needed. Make it your mantra. Tape it to a paper on your mirror. Talk to friends and ask them to pray for you. Be bold and specific in your requests. Repeat to yourself that you are loved. Pray for the Lord to take your heart captive and bombard you with His love. Wait for it. He will.

When you are feeling undeserving, I pray you know this love is a free gift we all have been given because the Creator of the Universe is Love. We were made by Love and we were created for Love to reside within us, to flow from us and through us. Not one of us is deserving of this gift, but it is one bestowed on all. When you are feeling undeserving, repeat this truth: "This love is a free gift given to all. It is the gift of love from Love.[4] It is not something I earn. It is not something deserved. It is my gift." Say it again: "It is my gift. It does not give as the world gives. It is eternally mine. No strings attached."

When you are feeling unredeemable, I pray you know that no matter how far you fall, there is a loving hand reaching down to pull you up. I have felt the loving hand of the Lord reach down many times in my life, and I have had to learn how to recognize that hand and grab hold. You can grab hold, too. When Jesus bowed His head and gave His Spirit for all creation, He took it all: Every pain. Every betrayal. Every loss. Every sin. He took it and declared, "It is finished."[5] When you are feeling unredeemable, repeat this truth: "I am redeemed by His scars. There is nothing in this world beyond redemption. All I need to do is lay it at His feet. I am redeemed."[6]

And if you feel as if too much time has passed, as if you have wandered through the desert for too long and have forgotten the faith that once shaped and formed you, remember, it's never too late to return. There is no amount of time that is too great and no hourglass keeping track of the sand that has fallen. Love has no time limit. You will always be welcomed, and His arms will always be extended and waiting.

Let God's love wash over you. Let it undo you. There is no greater love than the love God has for you. For me. For us. The world. Sit in that space for as long as needed.

Abide in His Presence.

You, my friend, are loved.

Rhythms of Return

Prayer

Giver of Love,

Undo me. Take all the lies that are twisted inside—the words of the enemy that tell me I am unlovable or unworthy—and replace them with this truth: I am loved. Your heart for me burns hotter than the heat of a thousand suns. Your compassion for me extends beyond the farthest galaxy. The number of strands of hair on my head, breaths I will breathe, and nights my eyes will close in slumber have been logged by You for all of time. Your thoughts of me stretch on for an eternity that is beyond my grasp.

You have held me under Your wing. You have reached for me and are reaching for me and will always be reaching. No matter how far I run. No matter how long it takes.

There is nothing to keep Your love away. Even when I don't listen. Even when I refuse to receive. Even when I run from You.

You are still there.

Help me to grab on, Lord. Help me take that truth to heart and return to it over and over and over in my day. Transform me. Bombard me. Captivate me.

I am loved. I am loved. I am loved.

Thank You, Jesus.

Amen.

Questions for Reflection

1. Do you believe in your heart that God loves you, as is, with no strings attached? If not, why do you think believing in His love is hard for you?
2. What are some of the lies you harbor in your heart? Do these lies keep you in a space of believing you are unlovable?
3. Love means a lot of things to a lot of people. What does love mean to you?
4. What are some ways you experience love? Ask God to reveal His love to you in tangible ways this week.

Invitation to Return

One Minute: Throughout this week, make *I am loved* your mantra. Tape it to your mirror. To the dashboard of your car. To the fridge. Use it as the background image in your phone. Repeat it over and over and over, and ask God to make this your truth. Saying the words won't take much time but will have a powerful impact on your heart and soul.

One Hour: Pick a special place where you can sit in quiet reflection. Play some peaceful music in the background or, if you prefer, sit in silence. As you sit, ask the Lord to fill you with His love. Feel it all around you and in you. Sit in that space, as uncomfortable as it may be, for as long as you feel led. Ask Him to show you what it means to be loved by Him. Embrace that love and let it take you captive. After you have spent time bathed in the love of the Lord, journal about your experience.

One Day: Reserve a day to be in the presence of the Lord. He is always there, inviting us to meet with Him, but it is so easy for the distractions of the day to rob us of the love we feel when we abide with Him. Decide in advance what that looks like. Is it sitting in a beautiful chapel? Hiking in the woods? Taking a trip to a local spa? Where can you go to simply *be*? Pray over this day in advance and trust His love will meet you there.

2

RETURN TO PEACE

An Anchor in the Chaos

Be still, and know that I am God.
—Psalm 46:10 (ESV)

When I was in third grade, my parents divorced. My mom, sister, and I moved into my grandparents' home while our small house across the pond was being built. It was a hard time in my life—a time when I felt like I was constantly moving through chaos and uncertainty. I didn't know what this new life would look like. I didn't know if I would fit in at this new school in this new town.

At the age of eight, I didn't have the emotional capacity to deal with all these new emotions that were swirling inside. The fear. The anger. The uncertainty. The longing for the life I had that would never be again.

As I was packing my room in a state of melancholy, my attention shifted to the closet. I stuck my finger in the small round hole on the door and slid it open to begin sorting and gathering my items. What I saw appalled me.

The closet was a mess. My toys. Art supplies. Clothes. Coloring books. All in piles and completely unorganized. Something that had never bothered me before suddenly felt unacceptable.

My closet looked the way my insides felt.

In that moment, I thought, *Never again*. Never again will my life get so messy. Never again will I lose control of my environment like this. There was much in life that was out of my control—my parents, my home situation, what school I would attend, even my emotions—but this? This I could control.

I was attempting to create peace in the chaos of my storm.

To this day, I remain a tidy, organized person. My bed is made first thing every morning. I have a menu for the week and a laundry schedule. Everything in my home has a place. I know where things are. I know what's for dinner. My surroundings are generally calm and orderly, but this doesn't provide the full life of peace I seek. While my soul cries out for that fullness, I won't find it in an ordered closet. I know this, yet I often trade in that soulful peace for the crushing weight and mental load of daily demands.

If someone asks how I'm doing, I respond with, "I'm good, just busy," followed by a laundry list of the things that are keeping me occupied: "I have to pay the bills, start the laundry, then head to the grocery store for the week. After that, I'll feed the kids, switch the laundry, and start a new load. Oh, and I have about a billion text messages, voxes, Marco Polos, DMs, Snaps, and emails that are begging for replies. And next week we have a birthday party, so I need to go shopping for supplies, get dinner ready, and buy wet food for the cats because you know the cats can't live without their wet food." Any of this sound familiar?

Friend, we are busy. We are harried. We are distracted. We are stressed. We are anxious. We are longing for a minute of peace in our chaotic lives, but we can't figure out how to make that a priority. Our calendars are overbooked, our children are young and in need of constant care, our work schedules are demanding, our parents' health is ailing, and we are supposed to be recording it all on our social feeds and stories—the list of to-dos is overwhelming and leaves us feeling exhausted and depleted.

It's all so demanding.

But peace isn't demanding. It is completely counter to all the noise swirling around us and the hundreds of directions we feel pulled in a day.

Peace is something you pursue in the midst. Peace is something you breathe in and exhale out. Peace is a way of being that requires intentional action (or inaction). Peace is something you move toward. Peace is countercultural. And it is what Jesus offers His children.

Return to Jesus

There is something magical about the early-morning hours that calls to my heart. I feel a sort of pull to rise before the sun and experience the quiet stillness in the air and the comfort that comes from knowing everyone is tucked snugly in their beds with covers pulled tight and heads resting on soft, downy pillows. To enjoy those early hours of prayer and reflection as my hands wrap around a mug of steaming-hot coffee with sweet cream, surrounded by my Bible and a stack of opened journals, acutely aware of my hopes for the day that stretches ahead. Those gentle mornings where the demands of life are held back by the peace Jesus promises.

His promise is clear. "Peace I leave with you; my peace I give you. I do not give to you as the world gives. Do not let your hearts be troubled and do not be afraid."[1]

The world gives chaos, yet Jesus gives peace.

Like those magical early mornings, you'll know when you

feel His peace. It surpasses all understanding. It doesn't fit with the chaos of the moment, yet it's there. The anxiety settles. Your breathing slows. The feeling is different from the rest of your day. It isn't demanding of your time and energy. It isn't pressing from the outside or pulling from the inside. His gift is like a warm blanket being offered on a cold night. It's the feeling of walking barefoot on the sand as the waters crash up against the shore, a refreshing bit of reprieve from the sweltering heat of a summer's day. It's like the atmosphere when your house grows quiet and everyone settles in for rest after a long and weary day. Only you don't have to wait for the blanket. You don't need to travel to the tropics. You don't have to wait for the silence to settle. That feeling. That moment. That calm. It's there. It may not feel like it when you are in the middle of the pressure, but Jesus's peace is reaching down for you, inviting you to take hold.

So when the daily grind kicks in and your sanity threatens to break, return to the Prince of Peace. You can accept the invitation to receive this precious gift by investing in your relationship with Jesus in the same way you do with anyone: by spending time with Him.

I know what you're thinking: *Okay, that sounds great. I want that and I've* tried. *But I struggle putting it into practice. How do I return to Him during the chaos of my day? How do I release my burdens and surrender them into His care?*[2] *How in the world do I find the time?*

I get it. I really do. Our consumer-driven, commercial environment of how-to manuals tells us that we can find the time, because surely anyone can wake up early, work out, read their Bible, make homemade bread, and shower, all before 6 A.M. But there is no one-size-fits-all solution.

I have had days when I would wake before my kids and husband and revel in the silence I desperately needed. While those early mornings restored my soul, they did not last. And no matter how hard I try, I cannot get the habit to stick. My alarm goes off and, in a state of exhaustion, I end up hitting snooze again and again until I have no choice but to finally respond because I have to get the kids out the door for another day of school.

So what happens when we have this idea of what we want our schedules, habits, rhythms, and practices to look like, and it's just not happening? What happens if we wake only to find that we didn't meet our early-morning goal—*again*? What happens if we have a vision for how we want our days to look and our spiritual life to look, or the way we think it's all *supposed* to look, and we just can't seem to make that vision a reality?

Do we feel worthless? Do we feel like a failure?

Do we throw up our hands in defeat? Do we give up?

No. We don't give up. We press forward. We find what works for us in this season of life, with its daily list of to-dos, mountains of laundry, endless dishes, people running in and out of the house as they grab a snack and the door slams behind—this season of life with demands piling. We meet with the Lord in ways that work. We become available and present throughout the entire day. We live the peaceful life God intends for us. Now. Here. Today.

So when I keep coming up against roadblocks to waking early—namely, a demanding schedule with teenagers who now keep me up late at night—I readjust. I pursue different disciplines that work for me and my family in the stage of life we find ourselves in right now. I learn to see the invitations that lie waiting for me all throughout the day. And I meet Jesus there.

In today's hurried season with four tween and teen children, a husband who is traveling more for work than ever before, an increased work schedule (hello, book!), and all the other things that press in, I meet Jesus at the kitchen sink, while folding laundry, in the car while I wait for the kids to come out of theater rehearsal, and in all the little moments throughout my day.

I know, I know: some of you may be thinking, *God deserves more than that.* And I agree. He deserves our everything, but the reality of life right now is that small snippets of time work for me. And I know that in whatever way I meet with the Lord, He is glad I am there. Whether for one minute, one hour, or one day, He rejoices that I have returned. He meets me in that space and He freely gives His peace.

I will let go of those things that do not work, and I will lean into those things that do. Because He longs for me to meet Him in the busy, in the demands of the world, and in the overwhelm. He isn't removed. He is very present through it all—waiting for me to commune with Him. As He waits for you, too.

You have a God who longs to meet with you in the sacred and the mundane, in the hurried and the calm. He longs to hear your voice, your thoughts, and asks you to "Never stop praying."[3]

Never. Stop. Praying.

That can feel a bit overwhelming, but the message being conveyed here is not that you spend all day on your knees in prayer, because that just isn't feasible (and would also lead to some serious knee and back issues). No, it's not that you shut out the world and stop interacting with everything and everyone else but Him. Rather, the idea is to learn to be in regular communion and relationship with God in the midst. It is about abiding *with* Him while you are moving through life. And that takes practice.

Maybe you go on walks where you practice being present with your environment and your God and simply listen. Or maybe you find yourself kneeling by the bedside at night, or first thing in the morning. Maybe you turn on worship music while the lunches are packed and breakfast is made. Maybe you grab your journal and jot down the ways you have seen God move. However you choose to return to Jesus, you will find peace in the busy. Your mind and body will slow, your breath will be restored. Your eyes will move from your circumstances to your Creator.

And as you shift your gaze from in and around to up, you will find restoration for your weary soul.

The Way of Peace

As I write this chapter, it is the season of Lent. Easter is just two short weeks away. As a child growing up Catholic, I remember fasting from one or two things for a month. This practice from my past was one I chose to let go of, but over time, I came to see the great value in fasting. When I picked up the practice again as an adult, I understood how it could turn my distracted eye to the Lord and saw it with a renewed, matured sense of awe. But, this year, I decided to do something different than just remove something I love.

I decided it wasn't just about the stripping away, but also about replenishing.

In addition to the fasting, I have intentionally added peace-giving rhythms into my day to help shift my eyes to the Lord. These rhythms help me to slow down, reorient, and return to what matters when the chaos comes swiftly and time with God gets squeezed out by the demands of the day.

Some of my daily Lenten rhythms include stretching, praying and meditating, keeping a gratitude journal, spending at least ten minutes outside, touching the earth in some way to ground myself to creation (I'm crunchy like that), and sending someone a message so they know I love them and am thinking of them.

While that list may sound like a lot, each of those things does not take long to complete. A minute here. A couple minutes there. Yet they require intentionality to step out of my "need tos" and "have tos." They take me out of my demanding schedule, slow me down, ground me in the present, and reorient my body, mind, and soul to the God of the Universe.

When I take a time-out to do these things, I am exchanging the hustle for the calm. I am releasing my daily burdens, if only for a couple minutes. This season of fasting has reminded me I can take out what is no longer needed and add the things that bring life to my day. I can remove the distractions. I can engage in actions that bring peace.

It requires me to turn off the autopilot way of life I can so often unintentionally find myself living, and instead live a life of intentionality. A life where I pursue calm in a world that asks me to never stop moving.

What about you? What ways can you sit with Jesus in this season to receive His peace? Perhaps you're able to wake early, spend time with the Lord, and reflect on the tasks ahead. Perhaps you can break during the day for a walk and find peace from the noise. Perhaps you can find ten minutes before bed to return to the sacred by writing a prayer for those you love. The key is to find what creates peace in the chaos you find yourself in today.

There are so many ways you can return to Jesus, and it is important to understand there is no right or wrong way to meet with Him. Find what works for *you*, and be flexible. Because what works now may not work as well in a week or two or three—and that's okay. And, like in my case with Lent, it may be time to pick up a practice from your past that once didn't work, but makes sense now. Find the rhythms of return to Jesus that fit your life; then, make it tangible.

Jesus longs to meet you in the worry: during the late-night feedings and in the wee hours while you wait for your teen to come home. He wants to commune with you in the busy: at the baseball game as you're scheduling the dentist appointments, and at the birthday party when you're serving cake to a throng of seven-year-olds. He wants to talk with you in the stress: when your work deadline is approaching and the papers on your desk are multiplying. He desires to pull you up and out of the mental load as you drive to help your ailing parent, try to figure out what's for dinner, and wonder how you will pay that unexpected bill.

So never stop praying. Learn to commune with the Lord in all things. Because the chaos will come. You can clean your closets and order your life to help when things feel out of whack and anxiety rears, but you'll need more than that to discover true inner peace. You'll need the Prince of Peace and the calm He desires for you.

As you move intentionally toward Him and release, surrender, and find rhythms that work for you, you'll abide in His presence and discover a peace that doesn't make sense in this world of self-sufficiency, keeping up with the Joneses, and the pressure of maintaining a Pinterest-board home and lifestyle. You'll discover a peace that passes all understanding.

Rhythms of Return

Prayer

Prince of Peace,

The world can feel so chaotic with demands pressing from all sides.

You see me squeezed, bent, and twisted. Trying to look up but head bowed toward within.

Untangle me from those circumstances that threaten to take hold.

Turn my gaze from within toward You.

I know Your holy is where I find my whole.

This is not lost on me.

Yet I try so hard to do it on my own.

I am not meant to do it on my own.

Pull me up and out of my chaos, and lay me on Your lap to rest.

Stroke my hair. Hold my hand.

Breathe peace into my spirit with Your Spirit Divine.

Peacemaker, empty me of the chaos.

Fill me with You.

Amen.

Questions for Reflection

1. Is there a habit or discipline you keep trying to make yours in this season that just isn't working for you? What if you lay that down and acknowledge it may

not be for you right now? How does that make you feel? If you feel any guilt, ask God to remove that guilt from you.

2. When in your life have you felt true peace?

3. When you think back to that time, what stands out to you? How did you feel? Is this something you have felt since?

4. I thought ordering my outside world would fix my inside, but that's only a temporary solution. Are there things you find yourself doing as a "quick fix" for peace? What is the difference in your life between this temporary satisfaction and the peace that comes from Jesus?

Invitation to Return

One Minute: Whisper His name in moments of chaos. Part of the return to Jesus is learning to acknowledge your relationship with Him in all things, which includes those moments when we may not feel Him with us. When the stress from daily pressures takes over, whisper His name. Do this as many times as needed. Say His name over and over in a rhythmic pattern. Breathe Him in and out and know He is with you in the calm of the day as well as in the chaos.

One Hour: Take time to pray about your daily routine. Ask God to show you different disciplines that are working, have worked in the past, or could work in the season you are in now. Take out a piece of paper and pen, and brainstorm the spiritual habits that come to mind.

One Day: Now, as a follow-up to your one-hour activity, pick one day this week to begin incorporating the spiritual habits you chose for this season. Ask the Holy Spirit to give you a deep soul desire to meet with God in these ways beyond just this one day. Ask Him to help you develop these rhythms of return into habits. Start with this one day and see where it will take you.

3

RETURN TO COMFORT

The World Has Stopped
and All Feels Shattered

Courage, dear heart.

—C. S. Lewis, *The Voyage of the Dawn Treader*

On August 12, 2008, my friend Jill, her daughter, Kylie, and our two daughters, Sophia and Amelia, were enjoying a couple days at my parents' lake home in northern Indiana. The day started off like any other: we rose, dressed, ate breakfast, then spent the morning blueberry picking. The girls had just laid down for an afternoon nap. Jill and I were doing what moms on a small vacation at a lake home do while their children are napping: enjoying fresh air and relaxing in the sun. Then the phone rang.

Ring.

Ring.

Ring.

Jill answered, and I could tell in an instant from her pained expression that this call was not good. Her husband, R. D., had been in an accident. He was working for a landscape company over the summer, and a lawnmower had fallen on top of his body and caught on fire. It was bad, and we had to go. We woke the girls, packed our bags, and headed out the door. I didn't know two moms with three small and sleepy children could possibly move so fast.

Tragedy has a way of propelling us like that.

On the three-hour car ride home, I drove while Jill was on the phone. She would say words like "burns covering most of his body" and then "paralyzed," with an audible gasp and a sob. How could a day of sun turn to darkness so fast?

My foot pressed harder on the pedal.

We finally arrived at the hospital where R. D. had been transported by the ambulance. I dropped Jill off at the entrance and simply said, "Don't worry about Kylie, we've got her."

As I watched Jill walk through the doors, I looked at the neighboring hospital and my mind rested for a minute on the fact that this was where Emily, one of my best friends since fourth grade, was recovering from her bone marrow transplant that had happened just a few hours prior.

I drove away with the three girls packed tightly in the back of our Avalon and did all I knew to do: I prayed.

I had no idea what the next months or years would hold, but I knew things were about to change in ways I could not imagine. And I knew I needed God in ways I had not needed Him before.

When I arrived home, my husband set up the Pack 'n Play for our five-month-old in our bedroom and a mattress for Kylie on the floor in the nursery. For the next few months, this became her room during most days and nights while Jill stayed by her husband's side at the hospital.

During this time, my friend Emily's bone marrow transplant resulted in graft-versus-host disease. Her body was being attacked, and her short stay in the hospital was now looking to be much longer than anticipated.

Weeks turned into months, and I would spend the days caring for the girls. Sometimes, taking Kylie to the hospital to visit her dad. Sometimes, finding someone to watch the kids for a couple hours during the day so I could sit by Emily's side. In the evenings, after dinner was served, baths were complete, and the kids were tucked safely in their beds, I would often go to be with Emily. And usually, at least once a week, I would make a bed for myself on the guest cot in her hospital room. I would wake in the wee hours of the night to pump milk for my nursing daughter, then rise early in the morning to get home before my husband had to head out the door for work.

Everywhere I went, there was more pain than my heart could bear. I tried to lean into the Lord. I knew He was there, but was He really?

A quiet voice whispered in the night and grew louder as days turned to weeks and to months: *Where are You, Lord? How could You possibly allow this to happen? I thought You were supposed to be good? Aren't You good, God?*

Have you been there? Perhaps you've suffered an unexpected diagnosis, a job loss, a broken relationship, or the death of someone you deeply love. These unforeseen moments stop your world, but the outside world doesn't slow down.

People continue to move in the same ways that they always have, day in and day out. The cars drive down the road. The kids wait at the bus stop to be picked up for another day of school. Parents push babies in strollers down the sidewalk next to teenagers riding on bikes while grandparents walk their dogs. The sun continues to rise and set as it always has. All those people doing all those normal things seems odd on a day when your normal has been shattered into a million tiny pieces.

You want to open your window and yell, "Today isn't a normal day. Don't you see? It's not a day for bike riding or heading to the grocery store in your car. Today is the first day of life never being the same again. The world has stopped. Don't you feel it? How can you not feel it?"

When we found out our daughter, Amelia, had a lung abnormality and there was concern she may have cystic fibrosis, the world stopped.

When my parents told me my dad would be moving out, never to move back in again, and then again, when my dad and stepmom declared their marriage was beyond repair, the world stopped.

When I was sixteen years young and my grandpa slipped on the ice and into a concussion he never would wake from, the world stopped.

When my father-in-law took his final breath after his battle with lung cancer ended, the world stopped.

When I heard the news that my cousin had died by suicide at the age of thirty-nine, the world stopped.

When the nurse asked to step out of the room for the ultrasound machine, then spoke one of my worst fears into existence: "There is no heartbeat. Your baby is dead," the world stopped.

The before and after in these world-stopping moments become some of the defining periods of our lives: the time before the life-altering event and everything that falls after. We pick up the pieces and try to put them back again, but no matter how hard we try to force them to fit together, this puzzle of life as we know it will never be the same.

And when our worlds have been turned upside down by something that is so full of pain and heartache, we may discover our faith being tested. We may wrestle with doubt. We may cry out to God in our anguish and say, "My God, my God, why have you forsaken me?"[1]

If you've ever experienced this soul-level doubt, then I have good news for you: God can take it. One of His chosen disciples was even nicknamed Doubting Thomas, because when Thomas saw Jesus after He had risen from the dead, Thomas had to touch the scars on His hands before he could fully believe.[2] Likewise, God can take your doubt and your pain and your heartache. He can take you waving your hands in the air at Him and even yelling at Him. You don't have to hide these emotions from God.

Because He knows. He knows what it is to feel. How can we be certain He knows? Because while He is fully God, He was also fully human and experienced the same breadth of emotions we all know so well. Jesus knows because Jesus lived.

Jesus was born from His mother, ran and played as a child, learned from His parents, and took up His calling as Rabbi. He walked among the people and the trees. He saw the birds fly, and His sandaled feet kicked up dirt on the ground. He sat at a table to eat and drink wine with those He loved.[3] He comforted friends in their pain after news of the loss of a loved one.[4] He wept.[5]

Jesus loved, and He was betrayed.[6] He took His final breath on the cross and was buried in a tomb. Fully human. And being fully human means, maybe at some point, in his humanity, Jesus felt His world stop, too.

Return to Jesus

Mary, Martha, and Lazarus were siblings and Jesus's dear friends. They had hosted Jesus and His disciples in their home. Martha had cleaned and prepared meals for Him. Mary had sat at his feet and listened to Him teach. These siblings loved Jesus, and He them. So when Lazarus fell deathly ill, the sisters sent for Jesus, saying, "Lord, the one you love is sick."[7]

The sisters trusted Jesus. They knew He loved Lazarus and, rightfully so, expected Jesus to hurry over. But Jesus didn't rush off:

When he heard this, Jesus said, "This sickness will not end in death. No, it is for God's glory so that God's Son may be glorified through it." Now Jesus loved Martha and her sister and Lazarus. So when he heard that Lazarus was sick, he stayed where he was two more days, and then he said to his disciples, "Let us go back to Judea."[8]

Jesus stayed where He was for two more days. Not a few hours. Not one day. *Two days.* Can you imagine receiving a call that your loved one was sick, possibly on their deathbed, and that they needed you? Most of us would drop everything and head out the door.

I often wonder how Martha and Mary felt while they waited. I wonder if they calculated how many days it would take until Jesus would receive their message, and how long it would be before He should have returned had He left immediately. I wonder what thoughts went through their minds in those two days as they were waiting. Did they doubt?

If they were anything like me, they would have been frustrated, anxious, and, perhaps, even annoyed. Maybe they questioned His love and if He really cared at all. "I ran to You. I called for You. What are You waiting for? Where are You? Why aren't You here already?"

But Jesus wasn't anxious. He wasn't concerned. He wasn't responding impulsively out of His own desires. Instead, He was doing the will of His Father and waiting for the proper time to go.

While Jesus was waiting to leave for Judea and the sisters were waiting for Him to answer their cries, Lazarus died. Four days after Lazarus had been buried, Jesus arrived:

> When Mary reached the place where Jesus was and saw him, she fell at his feet and said, "Lord, if you had been here, my brother would not have died."[9]

Mary and Martha's world stopped spinning. In her pain, Mary ran to Jesus and placed herself in a posture of surrender at His feet. And she wept. Crumpled, balled-up body, sobs of grief. She cried out, *Where were You? Why didn't You do something?* "Lord, if You had been here, my brother would not have died."

If. You. Had. Been. Here.

And what was Jesus's response? Was it to reprimand her for her lack of faith? Was it to tell Mary to stand up and trust Him? Was it annoyance that she had questioned His actions?

No. When Jesus saw Mary weeping and the Jews who had come with her weeping, He was not frustrated. He was not taken aback. He was not annoyed. He was deeply moved in spirit. He was troubled.[10]

Jesus wept.

And there it is—one sentence that is so powerful. One sentence that reveals the depth of love the Lord has for all of us. Two words that show the compassion Jesus feels for us in our moments of anguish.

The Greek word is "dakruó."[11] This kind of crying isn't the balled-up wailing kind, but the kind that is silent, yet immensely powerful. It is tears slipping down the cheeks of Jesus. Jesus was so moved with compassion that even though He knew the outcome of this story, He still cried. He cried with them. And for them. Because of His great love for them.

And then Jesus, still filled with compassion, moves. He goes to Lazarus's tomb and commands the stone to be removed:

> So they took away the stone. Then Jesus looked up and said, "Father, I thank you that you have heard me. I knew that you always hear me, but I said this for the benefit of the people standing here, that they may believe that you sent me."

When he had said this, Jesus called in a loud voice, "Lazarus, come out!" The dead man came out, his hands and feet wrapped with strips of linen, and a cloth around his face.

Jesus said to them, "Take off the grave clothes and let him go."[12]

This is such a mic-drop moment. Jesus has power over death. Lazarus, who was dead in the tomb, walks out. Can you even begin to imagine? Your loved one walking out of their grave wrapped in linen, with a cloth around their face? I confess, I probably would've been afraid, like I was witnessing something straight out of *Night of the Living Dead*[13] rather than a miracle. But even if that would have been my response, Jesus would love me all the same.

His love for us never wavers. Even in our doubt, our anger, our frustration, our fear, and our questioning. He loves us. Jesus feels compassion for us. Jesus knows what it means to have faith and yet still feel pain cut deep. He knows that so often our joy resides alongside our sorrow—two roads that seem so distant from one another but often intersect. Jesus has felt our pain. He weeps for us. And, just like Jesus continued to work before leaving for Bethany, God is working. Even if we think He has not heard our cries. Even if He seems silent. Even if we feel like we are waiting two days or an eternity to hear from Him. God is working. When Lazarus stopped breathing. When R. D. had the accident. When Emily was sick. In every world-stopping moment, God is working.

I have doubted God's work, His choices, and His will. I am confident I will doubt again. But my doubt does not come with guilt. It does not come with fear that God will be upset with me. I have come to see my doubt and wrestling as a beautiful, human part of the faith experience.

The Bible is full of doubters. Full of people questioning and asking God to do things He had just done a couple days ago or even a few minutes ago. These doubters walked with Jesus. They talked to Jesus. They were His friends and His faithful companions.

They saw Him multiply five loaves and two fish to feed the five thousand.[14] Then, not long after witnessing that miracle, they found themselves in the same situation again, asking Jesus where the food was going to come from to feed the four thousand they were facing this time.[15]

They were full of doubt.

Martha and Mary did not know what the Lord's plan was for their brother. When Jesus chose to delay His arrival, perhaps, for a moment, they felt the Lord had abandoned them. Perhaps they doubted. But Jesus knew the Father's plans and was operating from a place of trust. And when the time was right, He came to them. This doesn't mean that He wasn't always with them. Jesus was with them even when He seemed far away. What they hadn't realized about Him yet was that it wasn't just about His physical presence. He is the Father. He is the Son. He is the Holy Spirit, who is also referred to as the Comforter.[16] Three in one. The Godhead. This is the mystery of the presence of God.

Jesus had not abandoned them. He heard their cries. He felt their pain and wept with them. He comforted them. Then, according to His Father's will, Jesus answered their prayers. And when Lazarus walked out of the grave, the Divine was glorified.

Never Alone

I was with Emily the day before she died. I sat by her hospital bed with her children, husband, parents, and loved ones in the room. I told her how much I loved her and what she meant to me as she lay in the bed hooked up to tubes and machines with beeping monitors. I prayed the Lord would spare her. I went to bed that night believing He would, but in the morning, when I called her husband to ask if I could bring him a coffee, he said the words I never wanted to hear.

"Emily died last night."

My world stopped. I collapsed to the ground as cries of anguish escaped my lips.

Her death was agonizing for those of us left here. Many had prayed faithfully and consistently for Emily's healing, but that wasn't God's will for her life. Instead of physical healing on Earth, God chose to take Emily home to heaven. But to pray and believe with every fiber of our being that she would be healed, only to realize that prayer would not be answered, was heartbreaking.

Sometimes, your prayers will not be answered in the ways you hoped. Your story may not end with the Lord saying, "Take off the grave clothes and let him go." That may leave you feeling abandoned. But you are not alone. God is working. Your story is still being written. I know that doesn't take away the pain. Doesn't remove the despair you have felt in your world-stopping moment when your body crumpled to the ground and wails of grief escaped your lips. Doesn't change your circumstances. But my hope and prayer is that you will find comfort knowing that Jesus is coming. And while you wait for Him to reveal His will, you can return to Jesus with the certainty that He is with you. He is weeping with you. For you. Because He loves you.

My world stopped when Emily died. But while life looks different now than before she passed, with time, my life slowly started to move again.

They say time is a great healer, and I have found this to be true. The people we lose never leave us, but as the seconds turn to minutes, to hours, to days, the pain does start to subside. Instead of feeling a tsunami of grief that threatens to knock you down for days, the grief starts to come in smaller waves, until one day, you can get into the water again.

For a long time after Emily passed, I thought of her daily. I missed her. I wanted to talk with her. To hear her voice. To talk about her kids and their sports and what she was making for dinner, like we had for all the years before. The missing-her was consuming. And then, without warning or even an awareness, the consuming thoughts and feelings subsided. Instead of missing her all the time, I would miss her only when something would trigger the emotion. I would see someone who looked like her at the grocery store and feel the tug on my heart. Or something would happen with my children that I wished I could share with Emily. In those moments, the grief would come, but it didn't take as long for it to subside.

I didn't realize it, but my world was starting to spin again. I was finding joy. I was able to think of her with more laughter and smiles than with tears. Her memory slowly became more like floating in comfortable waters than drowning in the depths. I wanted to share the things she taught me. To talk about the memories we made. My feelings shifted from sorrow at the thought of having lost her to joy at the gift of having known her at all.

But it takes time. I had to move through the grief. And all these years later, the grief will still come, but I don't fear it. I know it is all part of the world-stopping-and-spinning process.

If your world has stopped, likewise, you will start to move again, but not in the same ways you did before. So allow yourself time and space to experience the loss and the grief that have come with that moment. And once you come to the other side of pain, there is even a chance that joy will come in the morning. When that joy comes, please know, my friend, that to feel that joy is not a betrayal of your grief. It does not mean you no longer care about what you lost. That joy means enough time has passed that you can now hold both. And until that moment, remember that God is with you in your pain.

When R. D. was in the hospital and Emily was sick, I gave myself permission to say, "This sucks." I would look at the pain swirling all around and think, *I don't want this in my life.* I would feel the heartache and think of the days leading up to that August day and cry out, "This isn't what I ever dreamed my life would look like." Even as those words were coming out of my mouth, God was still good. Because when He felt distant, I see now that He was close. He was with me when I dropped Jill off at the hospital and took Kylie. He was with me while I pumped milk for my baby in the cold hospital room. He was with me as I drove, heavy-lidded and filled with fatigue, back home to care for three small children after a nearly sleepless night on a cold cot in a beeping room. He was with me when I was crumpled and wailing after hearing the news of Emily's death.

He is with you.

When the weight of grief bulldozes you to the ground, you may be angry. You may feel alone as the tears cascade like a waterfall into puddles around you, but you most definitely aren't alone. Just like Mary and Martha and Lazarus weren't alone.

You are never alone.

And here is the thing you may be able to hear now (and it's okay if you are in a raw spot and not ready to hear this yet, I get that): God is for you. He isn't against you. He isn't mean. As we talked about in the first chapter, He is the embodiment of perfect love. Take every bit of love you have ever felt in your life, magnify that by all of eternity, wrap it around all the universe, cover everything and everyone and all of creation with it, and you will have the love of God.

His love is what I remind myself of and what I return to when I am at a place where I am ready to receive it. God is working all things out for His good and His glory, and His glory is perfect love. Just like my daughter Nylah couldn't see the car ahead of her, I can't see the big picture that is all of time, but my God can. He can make sense of things that make no sense to me. And even though He sees the picture that is beyond what we can ever see or comprehend with our small little minds focused on this little eyeblink of time we get to live in, He still grieves.

He still weeps.

When I am uncertain, that is where I find my certainty: in my God who knows. My God who understands. My God who has already been there.

Fully Jesus.

Fully human.

Find comfort in His understanding, my friend, because your world will stop again. You will be angry with God again. You will wrestle with the questions of why. You will yell at Him and spew words of doubt up to the heavens. You will weep. But you are in the comfort of One who has wept, too. His great love covers you in those moments. He has gone before you, even if you can't see Him. Of this, you can be certain.

The world stops.

The world spins.

And through it all, you are covered in Love.

You are never alone.

Rhythms of Return

Prayer

Omnipotent One,

You know all things. You have gone before me,
and You have seen every world-stopping moment I will
encounter. You have been there through it all. Ever
present. Ever loving. Ever full of Grace.

You walk me through the shadow of death.

You lead me by still waters.

You are my great comfort when I feel all is lost.

May I lean into the promise of Your comfort when
my world is shattered. May I take refuge in the shelter of
Your wings when I cannot find my way forward.
May I remember always that You are good, even when
my circumstances are not. May I remember the truth
of You when the truth eludes me.

My world may be full of pain, but You are all that
is Love.

May I press into Your goodness in times of trial and
learn to trust that while I may not like the road I am
traveling, that doesn't mean that joy won't come in
the morning.

Amen.

Questions for Reflection

1. Think of a time when it felt like your world stopped. How did you feel in that moment? Did you feel alone? Did you feel God's presence with you?
2. Think of when your world started to move again. Was it hard to embrace your new normal? Are you still struggling to embrace it?
3. When have you experienced doubt? What did you do with that doubt? Do you feel you can take it honestly to God?
4. Do you feel God can handle your emotions? Even the negative ones? How does knowing that bring you comfort in times of struggle?

Invitation to Return

One Minute: Connect with how you feel emotionally. Don't be afraid of the negative emotions. Offer what you are feeling today to the Lord in prayer.

One Hour: Get out a piece of paper and write down all the moments when it felt like your world had stopped. Write how you felt in those moments and how you feel now after time has passed. Is there a common theme you notice? Did you doubt Him? Do you still struggle with doubting Him since these things have happened? End this time with honest prayer. Tell the Lord how you feel. Give it all to Him. Your anger. Your doubt. He can take it. And He wants to.

One Day: World-stopping moments are unpredictable and guaranteed. But you don't need to live in fear of those moments. Instead, you can trust in the One who goes before you and is with you in all things. Part of trusting comes as you see how He has been with you before. Pick a day and time to ask God to reveal to you His presence in a world-stopping moment. Once you know when that will be, pray over that time. Ask others to pray for you, too. When the day comes and you are ready to begin, make the room and space as peaceful as possible. Light candles, turn down the lights, play worship or instrumental music—whatever calms your soul. Ask God to show you where you were during that event and how He was with you. Ask Him if there is still healing that needs to take place. Revisiting those world-stopping events with God may be hard and may feel strange, but you can trust He will stay with you in that space and that healing will take place.

4

RETURN TO GRACE

Guilt Will Not Define Me

And the real mystery of grace is that it always arrives in time.
Like the wind, grace finds us wherever we are and won't leave
us however we were found.

—Ann Voskamp, *One Thousand Gifts*

I love summer break, especially as my kids have grown older
and sleeping in has become a reality again. (For those of you
with little ones: one day, this will be your reality, too. Promise.)
At the end of each school year, I look forward to the open schedule and lazy couple of months that stretch ahead. Yes, summer
is good to me. Except when I mess up.

Years ago, the first day of break started off as any other summer day.

The kids woke up and we wandered downstairs—some of us
full of energy, others still groggy-eyed and heavy-lidded (that
would be me). Breakfast was made, something was on the televi-
sion, and the day began as usual. A little after breakfast, the
bickering began.

This wasn't part of the plan. I could feel the blissful summer
day I had imagined slipping away. As the kids argued and I
broke up fights and disagreements, my internal temperature
started to rise. I was on the verge of boiling over.

Where was the rest? Where was the peace?

As I was slowly growing more and more frustrated and impatient, another argument broke out in the family room. I flew in to find two of my children arguing next to a pile of papers that had been wadded up, torn apart, and covered in a slew of pencil holes. It was a paper mutilation. On closer examination, I realized it wasn't one of their coloring books that had undergone this destruction for no apparent reason.

It was one of mine.

Do you know the kind I'm talking about? The coloring books for grown-ups with the intricate designs and detailed patterns that are supposed to help us relieve stress and attain some level of peace and satisfaction? Yes. Those coloring books. Maybe if I had been using it that morning instead of walking around picking up messes and cleaning the kitchen while listening to bickering, I would have found myself in a better headspace when I rounded the corner to see my children surrounded by this pile.

But I had not been coloring. And they hadn't been doing much coloring, either. Instead, they seemed set on destroying something, and my coloring book just happened to get in their way.

This was *my* coloring book. The one *I* received for Christmas. They had so many of their own. Why did they need mine? Was nothing of mine sacred? Was nothing off-limits? What. Happened. To. Personal. Space?!

Boil. Boil. Boil.

Overflow.

The lecturing began (which is a nice way to say yelling): "You have your own coloring books! Why did you have to use mine? And why did you destroy it? It's not nice to ruin other people's things! How would you feel if someone did that to your things? That's not very nice!"

I looked down on the floor and saw one colored picture amid

the wreckage. After my self-righteous speech about how you treat other people's things with respect, I looked my children in the eyes, reached down to the ground, and picked up the picture. Never breaking eye contact, I began my own path of destruction.

Boil. Boil. Boil.

Rip. Rip. Rip.

I tore the carefully colored masterpiece to shreds. Just like they had the pages in my book.

An eye for an eye.

The realization of my irrational actions stopped me hard. I went from boiling to complete remorse. *What had I done?*

What happened to turning the other cheek? Even worse, what impact would this eye-for-an-eye parenting have on my children? Guilty thoughts rattled around my brain. Then horrible feelings flooded my insides.

My daughter began to cry, her torn artwork lying in pieces on the floor around us. I began to cry as my eyes followed hers to the aftermath of my anger and frustration. Usually, you can't see the aftermath of the internal boilover, but I could see it. There was no turning away. There it was. I had let it all get the better of me. I reacted out of anger and not love.

All over a silly coloring book.

I knelt and opened my arms. My daughter jumped into them. I apologized and asked for her forgiveness. I explained how I was upset, but that didn't give me permission to destroy her beautiful artwork. We talked about how two wrongs don't make a right and held each other as the tears rolled down both of our cheeks.

After we embraced, I walked with her to the kitchen drawer where we kept the scotch tape. We picked up the artwork and pieced it back together. What was broken was made new again.

I'm not sure if my daughter even remembers that interaction

in the family room close to a decade ago, but it's one that is etched deeply in my mind. I have turned this mistake over to God and am confident I am forgiven—both by my daughter and by Him—yet I still pick it back up. I relive that moment in my mind over and over again. I watch as I rip my daughter's drawing to pieces. I feel the pang of failure as the guilt sinks into my heart.

Do you have moments in time you wish you could do over? The scene starts on mental replay and you wish you could jump back in time and yell to yourself, "Stop! Right now! Don't take another step forward! Don't say another word!"

But you can't. That thing happened.

We don't own a flux capacitor or a DeLorean, and time doesn't work like that.[1] So there's no rewriting history. And, as much as I wish we wouldn't, we will fail again. At some point, we will not choose wisely. We will lose our temper or say something we wish we could take back or act in a manner we had hoped we wouldn't. Not just with parenting, but with all things. At work. In marriage. With extended family and friends.

But do you know what? In the wake of the destruction, we may unintentionally, or intentionally, leave. In the ways we hurt others or hurt ourselves. In the poor choices we make. In the guilt that lands squarely on our chests after a moment we wish we could take back—like piles of torn papers and tear-soaked eyes of wounded children. We are forgiven. Not once. Not twice. But always.

Return to Jesus

There is no limit to God's forgiveness. Nor will there ever be. Jesus will never look down and say, "Well, that's it. We've tried. You just aren't going to cut it." That's what the world may say, but not our Heavenly Father. He knows all the things we will do, all the choices we will make, and all the ways we get turned upside down and boil over into the spaces we occupy—and still, He pursues us. Still, He forgives us. Through Jesus, we are freed from our mistakes:

> In him we have redemption through his blood, the forgiveness of sins, in accordance with the riches of God's grace.[2]

The riches of God's grace. Not the scarcity of God's grace. *The riches.*

But how often do we choose to exchange the riches for rags? How often do we choose to carry the boulder of our mistakes instead of walking lightly, arms swinging, free from the load?

When we go through the act of forgiveness, the guilt of those choices are no longer ours to carry. Even so, I sometimes struggle with completely moving on. I lay down the guilt, give it to Jesus, but I pick it back up again. I lose my temper or act unkindly, and the guilt slithers back in. I make a mistake and label myself: bad parent, unworthy friend, ungrateful child, lazy employee. Instead of looking at this as a new, isolated incident, I stack all my wrongdoings on top of each other. I forget I have been forgiven before and try to jump right back into that ooey, gooey mess when I've already been freed of it.

God doesn't want me stuck in those places. He wants me to freely walk with arms wide open and a heart filled with grace. One of my favorite verses, Galatians 5:1, says it best: "It is for freedom that Christ has set us free. Stand firm, then, and do not let yourselves be burdened again by a yoke of slavery."

Jesus came to set us free from sin, mistakes, and guilt. And when I confess my sin, I am forgiven. I am not defined by my past mistakes. I am not bound by my guilt. I am free.

Walking in freedom begins with claiming truth. For example,

I am not a bad mom. I know I am a good mom, but sometimes the enemy whispers lies into my ear, "You are a bad mom. Only a bad mom would tear up her daughter's artwork." However, if I were really a bad mom, I wouldn't care about being a good mom. If I were really a bad mom, I wouldn't feel remorse for those times I've messed up. Just like the times when I think I'm a bad wife, or a bad friend, or a bad coworker or employee. I'm not bad, I just messed up, because the truth is, I am an imperfect person raising imperfect humans in desperate need of a savior.

So I lay the guilt back down. I return to Jesus and repeat to myself, "It is for freedom that Christ has set me free." I exchange the lie and the label for the truth: I am a good mom who made a poor choice. I am forgiven. I am loved.

Walk in the Freedom of Jesus

Life is messy. We have stories of actions we wish we could take back. Things we wish we wouldn't have said or done. Ways that we wish we hadn't behaved. But we don't need to let our mistakes define us. We can embrace the truth that we are human in a world full of imperfect people doing imperfect things, reaching and trying and striving but never getting it fully right all of the time.

Only One has ever been perfect, and His sandaled feet walked the dirt roads over two thousand years ago. He traveled with disciples, and people flocked to hear His words. His sacrifice allows us to release the guilt and leave it at the cross. To say with confidence, "It is for freedom that Christ has set me free."

What are you holding on to that has you bound to the past? Are you ready to accept God's invitation to return to Him? To acknowledge the lies that are holding you hostage and replace them with the truth that Christ has set you free? If you are still wrestling with the guilt or self-imposed labels, then seek help from a trusted friend to hold you accountable and check in with you on how you're doing with the release. If the lies persist, then spend time asking God to change your heart and help you to see yourself the way He sees you. The more time you spend in His company, the more natural letting that guilt go will become.

As you accept the invitation to return to Jesus, you'll recognize the burden when it lands, and you'll know what to do with it. You'll actively lay down the guilt because you were never meant to hold the weight of it. You'll take the lies about your messes and measure them up against what God says. Then you'll replace them with the truth of who you are to Him. When you return to Jesus, you'll walk in freedom.

Freedom from the pressure to be perfect.

Freedom from the pressure to get it all right.

Freedom to be messy.

Freedom to let go of the guilt and the labels.

Freedom to walk in the light of His truth.

Freedom to keep moving forward in grace.

Freedom to lay it down and let it go.

Once and for all.

Freedom, when you return to Jesus.

Rhythms of Return

Prayer

Perfect One,

Help me to rest in Your presence and to embrace the fact that perfection is not what You ask of me. Help me to resist the labels I wear that were never mine to put on.

Unworthy. Failure. Mess-up. Incapable.

All the words I heap on top of myself, eyes closed to the gift of grace You daily bestow on me.

When guilt threatens to take hold, swiftly grab it from me. Show me the truth.

I am imperfect, and I am worthy. I mess up, but I am not a failure. I am not incapable. I am capable of change.

I am full of grace given with no limit by the One who knows every mistake I will ever make and loves me nonetheless.

When I do the thing I never wanted to do and say the words I never wanted to say, when grief and tears fall heavy, wipe my tears and remind me to walk lightly in this world. For always and forever.

Amen.

Questions for Reflection

1. What is a lie you believe about yourself or an unhealthy label you claim?
2. What is the truth you need to replace that lie or label?

3. What does it mean for you to lay something at Jesus's feet?

4. Is there something you have given to Him that you keep trying to pick back up? What about that is hard for you to let go of?

Invitation to Return

One Minute: It's time to take those thoughts captive. Place a jar somewhere in your home with small pieces of paper or a notepad and a writing utensil next to it. When you start placing labels on yourself throughout the week, write those thoughts down and place them in the jar.

One Hour: Empty the jar with the labels you have worn this week and replace them with truth. Look up scripture about who you are to the Lord. Meditate on the truth of how He sees you. Write down who you really are as His child, and discard those lies you have believed and the labels you have worn.

One Day: Go back to question three. What does it mean for you to lay something at Jesus's feet? If what you wrote included an action, schedule sacred time to complete that task, knowing God will meet you there. If what you wrote didn't include an action, then it's time to get creative. Create a visual reminder of the cross and the redemption that comes from the life of Jesus. Place it somewhere in your home where you will see it often. Use this visual as a daily reminder to walk in freedom and continue giving it all to the One who came to take it all.

5

RETURN TO RESTORATION

Put On Your Oxygen Mask

As you grow older, you will discover that you have two hands,
one for helping yourself, the other for helping others.

—Maya Angelou

Want to know a little secret?

Multiple nights a week, my husband fills a ramekin with peanut butter, covers it in chocolate chips, then heats it in the microwave to the point where it melts. He doesn't heat it so long that it's like soup, but just enough so you can still find that little crunch from the chocolate chips here and there. Then, he tops this ooey-gooey-chocolatey-peanut-butter deliciousness with a giant glob of whipped cream. He introduced this "peanut butter surprise," as he lovingly calls it, to my life many years ago, and it has brought a whole lot of joy to my heart—and my tastebuds—but maybe not so much my waistline.

Is your mouth watering? Mine, too.

And to make this sweet treat that much sweeter, my kind and loving husband makes and delivers it to me while I lay on the couch with my feet propped up, watching *Chopped* on the Food Network at the end of the day. Sometimes he will even ease down on the couch next to me and rub those feet of mine.

I used to feel kind of guilty about this routine. Like maybe I was being selfish accepting this nightly gift.

Not anymore.

Now, I kick back, hold out my hands and, with a smile on my face, say, "Thank you very much." Then I pick up the spoon and dig in.

Because I know that when I receive this kind gesture from my husband, savor something delicious, and watch a show I love, I fill my tank. This life-giving rhythm of self-care reorients me and allows me to pause and breathe. It's a moment for me to shut down, rest, and give thanks.

But coming to this place of rested acceptance took me a while. I struggled with accepting this rest, this beautiful picture of grace, without guilt attached. A few years ago, if I had heard this story from someone else, then I would have cheered them on from the sidelines. I could see the value of others taking care of themselves, but I couldn't accept that self-care was okay for me, too.

I was a stay-at-home mom to four children, all roughly two years apart. Can you imagine grocery shopping with babies, toddlers, and preschoolers in tow? A simple trip to the store for milk was not simple at all, and at that time, there were no grocery pickups or delivery services. I had to bring all four kids. Four voices yelling to buy them fruit snacks or Pop-Tarts or anything else loaded with sugar and dyes of every color. Four bodies to watch so they didn't toddle off and disappear. Four individual people to appease and tackle emotional breakdowns in the middle of the store—because you other mothers know temper tantrums are going to happen. It. Was. Hard.

Early on in our marriage, I had erroneously told myself that my job was to take care of the kids and everything that happened in the home: watch the kids, clean, buy groceries, run errands, make plans, keep schedules, pay the bills, do the laundry, cook food, and so on. While my husband's job was to work, play with the kids when he came home, mow the lawn, take out the trash, grill the steak—you know, manly things.

No one told me this was my job. Not my husband, not my friends, not my church—no one. In fact, my husband was always asking to help and telling me he was available, but I had a hard time accepting it. As an overachiever and recovering perfectionist who no longer received a performance review, I made this truth my own. This was my *job*.

And when I have a job, I do it well. Even if it kills me.

Well, life did what life does, and I learned my take-on-all-the-tasks-and-don't-ask-for-help process wasn't working. I was grumpy. I was tired. I was getting angry at the kids simply for being kids while I was running them from here to there on errands. I wasn't operating at my best. I was at about a one on the self-love and self-care meter, and something had to change.

I had to remove that big ball of pride I had unknowingly swallowed and humble myself. I had to ask for help. I had to learn that I didn't need to do all the jobs and that I could ask for assistance. I had to figure out how to advocate for my self-care.

After talking with my husband, he started going to the grocery store after the kids were tucked into bed. While he was shopping, I would lie on the couch or finish something at the house. He also started coming home to help me with the kids' daytime appointments, especially when someone unexpectedly got sick. On those nights, he would head back to work to make up hours missed during the day. Through a beautiful dance of give and take, we found a schedule that worked for us.

I learned to love myself. I asked for help, took alone time for myself, and accepted rest after a day of nursing babies and chasing toddlers. And as the dance shifts and seasons change, I continue to extend a hand of gratitude for the peanut butter surprise my husband hands me. Because I am worthy of love and care. And you are, too.

Do you feel other people are worth this kind of love, and encourage it in their lives, but sometimes—whether you realize it or not—have a hard time accepting the same kind of love for yourself?

You encourage those you love to rest, eat well, take time off, celebrate their wins, and do the things they love. You cheer alongside family and friends when they experience a victory, and you rush to their aid with meals, free babysitting, and words of encouragement when life throws them a curveball. You give support and are quick to affirm the good you see in them: "You look amazing," "You deserve to rest," "Enjoy your vacation," "You do you." You cheer on their social media posts when their feet are propped on hammocks or their toes are buried in the sand. Because we're all about the people in our lives taking care of themselves and living their best lives, aren't we?

But when it comes to encouragement and love and words of affirmation for yourself, do you feel the same? Do you offer yourself the same grace you are so quick to offer others?

When you rest, take time off, and do the things you love instead of being "productive," do you label yourself as lazy? When things don't go according to plan and unexpected life events throw you off, do you feel like you've failed? When your day, or week, or month, or year didn't produce the results you'd hoped for, do you see yourself as unworthy? When your life is so busy that you feel like you are drowning in your lists of to-dos and barely keeping your head above water, does the negative self-talk take over and leave you feeling depleted, lonely, and defeated?

Do you have a hard time asking for help?

Friend, why in the world are we so hard on ourselves? We

deserve to be cared for just like everyone else we love. You may not be one to love chocolate or the Food Network or even lounging on the couch, and that's totally okay if those aren't your things, but we all deserve rhythms of rest. We deserve comfort, relaxation, joy, a reprieve from the demands pressing in—whatever it is our souls may need. Even if we don't believe we're deserving of these things, we most certainly are. We deserve to love ourselves.

Wait. *Love ourselves?* What does that even mean? Aren't we supposed to be God-focused and family-focused and others-focused? Yes, yes, and yes. You're supposed to do those things, but to love others well, you also must embrace the love God wants you to have for yourself.

Return to Jesus

Does the thought of loving yourself make you feel a little squeamish? Does it make you uncomfortable to think of loving and caring for yourself? Maybe it even feels prideful or wrong to imagine elevating your needs in any moment above another's?

What if I were to say it's not prideful, but a show of humility? What if I were to say it's not wrong, but beneficial for everyone you encounter, when you care for yourself?

If this isn't sitting quite right within you, give yourself grace. The message of "run the marathon until you collapse without ever stopping for a replenishing glass of water" is one we can easily pick up in our culture where doing and giving are more popular and celebrated than resting and receiving. It can take a lot of untangling to accept this truth and live it out.

Friend, we have been called to live in an otherworldly way. We have been called to view all of God's creation through His loving lens. And that includes yourself. Matthew reveals that even Jesus cares about the love we have for ourselves:

Hearing that Jesus had silenced the Sadducees, the Pharisees got together. One of them, an expert in the law, tested him with this question: "Teacher, which is the greatest commandment in the Law?"

Jesus replied: "'Love the Lord your God with all your heart and with all your soul and with all your mind.' This is the first and greatest commandment. And the second is like it: 'Love your neighbor as yourself.' All the Law and the Prophets hang on these two commandments."[1]

When we read this verse, we often focus on the obvious statements: love God and love our neighbor. Okay. Makes sense. But don't miss the nuance of how we love our neighbor: love your neighbor *as you love yourself.*

Let that soak in for a minute because you may be thinking that loving yourself is selfish or wrong, but it isn't. You are as much a child of the Creator of the Universe, the Mover of Mountains, and the Great I Am as the people you are focusing on. It may be hard to believe, but it's true. Like we talked about in chapter one, God loves you with a ferocity you cannot comprehend. He wants you to take care of yourself, to love yourself, just like you long for those you love to be cared for.

God sees your to-do lists filled to the brim. He knows your unique struggles and empathizes with your pain and hurt. He is cheering you on when you're victorious, and He is rushing to your side when life doesn't go as planned. He yearns for you to rest, eat well, and make healthy choices. He wants you to have supportive, kind relationships with people who bring out the best in you. He longs for you to discover and use your gifts, passions, and talents. He wants you to love yourself well because He loves you.

When you see yourself as God sees you, recognize the value you bring to the table, and know you are worthy of good things, then you'll begin to see that taking time out of the day to replenish your soul is not selfish but, in fact, very good. You'll look for ways to fit self-care into your routine. And as you find rhythms of self-care, you'll gravitate toward the One whose love gives you space to breathe.

But I do realize this all can feel a bit abstract and hard to incorporate into our lives. The act of recognizing that God wants us to love ourselves may be easier to grasp than the notion of putting it into practice. So let's talk about two rhythms that you can use to begin actively loving yourself, because it's important, friend. And something each and every one of us needs in our lives.

Positive Self-Talk

When we look at those we love, especially those in our care, we can so easily say, "Yes! You should love yourself. Look at how incredible you are!" But do we say the same when we gaze at our reflections in the mirror? Do we look at ourselves and see the good within, or are we focused primarily on the negative and those things we wish we could change?

- If only I lost a few pounds. I wish I were younger. I have so many wrinkles. I will never look like her. I am so ugly.
- If only I were more interesting. Or funnier. Or had witty remarks to make in conversation. It's amazing anyone likes me.
- If only I had more money in the bank. My house isn't big enough. My car is too run-down. My clothes are so shabby. I am so behind on where I should be in life.
- I am such a bad friend. When was the last time I called somebody? When was the last time somebody called me? I am not sure I really matter to anyone.

Do you ever talk to yourself this way? What if you heard the people you love talking about themselves this way? Wouldn't you be quick to put a stop to all that negativity? Yet, when it comes to our own self-talk, we are quick to hurl insults.

Part of loving yourself is identifying and stopping the negative patterns of self-talk. Instead of putting yourself down, give yourself the grace you offer others; then take those negative thoughts captive and replace them with the truth about who you are. You are:

- Chosen, royal, and holy. You are called into His wonderful light.[2]
- Fearfully and wonderfully made.[3]
- God's temple, and God's Spirit dwells in you.[4]
- Loved.[5]
- A new creation.[6]
- Healed.[7]
- Redeemed.[8]
- An ambassador for Christ.[9]
- A friend of God.[10]
- Blessed.[11]
- The salt of the earth.[12]
- The light of the world.[13]

As you begin to replace the negative self-talk with truth, the crushing weight of condemnation that is often followed by the need to perform better or look a certain way or reach a certain social status or please others will be lifted. As you walk and bask in the light of the truth of who you are, *as you are*, your life will be transformed in ways you never dreamed possible. Instead of living with the constant pressure to achieve more, do better, work harder, strive, strive, strive, without ever taking a moment for yourself, you can lay all that down and pick up truth. You can silence the lies that are made to hold you down, and you can lift your arms and receive the goodness of God and the truth of who you are to Him.

God doesn't care about the size of your house or the money in your bank account. He isn't concerned with your reflection in the mirror. He doesn't need you to be the life of the party or the most entertaining person in the room. He isn't paying attention to the number of contacts saved in your phone or likes on your social feed. The world may measure our lives by these things, but the Lord asks us to let those pressures go and receive something so much better.

It is time to return. To know we are One with Him and that when He made us, it was not on accident. You were created for a purpose, and that purpose is good. And you, my friend, deserve to be loved and cared for. By others. And by yourself.

Active Self-Care

As I mentioned earlier, I am a creature of structure that was born from a need to control my outside environment. As I have healed, though, the habits and structure and schedules have become a form of self-care. They have kept me focused and grounded and allowed me to build space in my days to do things that bring me joy and fill my cup—like spending time with Jesus, working out, reading, or catching up with a friend over a steaming-hot latte. And sometimes, my curated days helped me more than I realized.

When my children were young, we stuck to a (mostly) strict schedule. I knew, for the most part, when they would wake, eat, play, and go down for naps, which also meant I knew when a small break was coming in my day. I have always loved art and knew I wanted this passion back in my life. But taking time to go to an art class wasn't an option for me, so I looked for another outlet. With only one income and four children, we didn't have a lot of extra money to buy new furniture, so while the kids were asleep, I would bring old pieces of furniture into the garage to paint.

Every day at nap time, I lifted the paint-soaked brush to each table and chair and breathed new life into these old pieces while they breathed life into my soul. I chose paint colors that brought joy to my eyes and watched the piece transform from a state of distress to beauty, just like my soul. With each stroke of the brush, I felt the stresses of the day release. It was a reset button for my emotions. I would breathe slower, almost rhythmically. Up. Breathe. Down. Breathe. Up. Breathe. Down. Breathe. There was new color. There was new life.

I soon found that painting old furniture wasn't the only thing that filled me. Whether I read, jogged, wrote, swam in the lake, danced with friends, or kicked off my shoes and walked barefoot on the grass, I was filled with joy and felt ready to take on the day.

The more I recognized my needs and gave myself permission to meet them, the more connected I became with my loved ones and God. I was more patient and present with my children because I had the breathing space to release irritations from earlier in the day. I grew closer with my husband because I wasn't greeting him from a state of complete depletion and complete exhaustion when he walked through the door.

As I loved on myself, my eyes moved from "do, do, do" to my God above. In the stillness and the pause, I found Him waiting for me. He had always been there, just as He always is. Waiting with tenderness for me to cast my gaze upon His face so that He could replenish my mind, body, and soul with the fullness that comes from the gift of His presence.

In this world, I may find myself blinded by the hustle, confusion, drive for success, envy, frustration, comparison, and all those things that come to rob me and my time here on Earth from living as salt and light, from living as a reflection of God. But when my eyes move to the eternal and I love myself as He loves me, I allow space for pause and replenishment. And in that space, there is a quiet that comes miraculously and majestically—like the slow and awe-inspiring glare of the sun as it moves from the sky down to the horizon, leaving more color in its wake than we knew the sky could hold.

As I loved myself, I better came to see what I have been continuing to learn all along, what this book began with: I am loved.

Friend, as you begin to love yourself as He loves you, I pray you better know this love, too.

The rhythms of self-care you incorporate into your day will look different from mine. You may rise early or sleep in. You may work out or choose to rest. You may search for creative outlets or go to places where you can enjoy the creativity of others. You may steal away quiet moments in the day. Or you may gather with friends for coffee and wine and meals and games. You might go on hikes or binge-watch your favorite shows on a streaming network while eating peanut-butter-chocolate goodness from a warm ramekin. Whatever you choose, find the time in your schedule to breathe life into your soul, connect to your Maker, rest, and be filled with His joy and love.

What rhythms of self-care have you built into your day? Do you schedule intentional breaks, or have you formed habits that create unintentional moments of self-care? Perhaps self-care has been a part of your life for so long that you've overlooked it, as I did with my scheduled days. As you start to recognize and acknowledge your acts of self-care, remember to give thanks for them and understand the good they bring into your day. Protect them and make them a priority, because they benefit not only you but also your relationship with God and those around you. And remember, the way you care for yourself will change based on the season you are in.

Self-care may be nearly impossible in some seasons. For example, life with a newborn or serving as a caregiver for someone else may make self-care more challenging. Maybe you've received a difficult diagnosis and you're walking through a new normal. Maybe your marriage has ended and you are at home caring for all the things by yourself that you and your spouse once cared for together. These are the seasons when self-care looks like letting others care for you. It may feel foreign, but allowing someone else to step in and help is a great way to keep filling your cup so that you are not operating from depletion, but rather from healthy spaces.

Allow others to step in and help. Extend your hand to every "peanut butter surprise" that's offered. The give and take is a beautiful dance to behold. Because when you love yourself, God's love overflows from your soul and rushes toward your neighbor, equipping you to "love your neighbor as yourself."

The Overflow of Self-Care

When we're on an airplane, the flight attendant instructs us to put on our oxygen mask first before helping others. The reason is simple: we need air to fill our lungs before we can help someone with the air in theirs. If we don't take care of ourselves first, everything and everyone around us can suffer, too. Remember the whole torn-paper incident?

I have caused my loved ones to suffer when I snap because I am exhausted and haven't taken a moment for myself. I have responded in haste to someone because my day is so overbooked that I don't even have an extra minute to say hello. When I haven't cared for myself, I have been more quick to judge, respond in anger, or not respond at all. But when I intentionally pause from the daily grind, turn my focus from the productivity to rest, and care for myself, then I'm filled with God's grace and love. My lungs are full, and I can help the person next to me.

When you take care of yourself, you're better equipped to deal with the many things life throws at you. Instead of trying to pour from empty, you pour from full. And when you pour from full, you have so much more to offer.

Instead of snapping at your loved ones, you may find your words and actions filled with more grace. Instead of running past someone at the pickup line because you are just too exhausted to say hello, you may find the energy to build relationships. Instead of responding in anger or judgment or silence because you are near the point of boiling over, you may find your cup so full that you are spilling goodness and kindness everywhere you go.

Love yourself, friend. Cheer for yourself. Check your oxygen supply frequently so you can live your best life and, in turn, be more mindful of God and others. Ground yourself in your rhythms of care. Rest when you need it. Return to Jesus and watch your focus move from the world to the eternal. Begin to see yourself through His lens. *Chosen. Royal. Holy. Called into His marvelous light. Fearfully and wonderfully made. God's temple, and God's Spirit dwells in you. Loved. A new creation. Healed. Redeemed. An ambassador for Christ. A friend of God. Blessed. The salt of the earth. The light of the world.*

Let go of the lie that our culture of independence wants you to believe: that we need to do it all by ourselves. Embrace rhythms of self-care without guilt or shame. It's time to live your best life now.

Your cup is filled.

And your cup overflows.

Your oxygen mask is placed on your face as you breathe in His truth and live out your rested life of joy.

Rhythms of Return

Father God,

May I fully embrace this love You have for me. May I love myself fully and completely and see that I am worthy of joy and rest and whatever else it is my soul may need as I travel through the valleys and the mountaintops of my life.

May I learn to love myself as I love others.

And the more I am engulfed in this current of love between You and me and those around me, may I be propelled to operate out of that love at all times and in all things.

As I am swept into the force of that love, may joy overtake my soul.

Help me to stop the negative self-talk.

Help me to make space for the gifts that lie waiting in my life.

Help me to embrace these rhythms and habits of self-care and self-love without guilt and with unapologetic joy.

And may these rhythms be contagious. May they give others around me permission to do the same. May I cheer others on toward living their best lives here and now.

Father and Giver of all good gifts, may I love myself as You do. Now and forever.

Amen.

Questions for Reflection

1. Is embracing the idea of loving yourself hard? Do you struggle with feeling like you need to be worthy? If so, why do you think this is hard?
2. In the season of life you find yourself in, what are some things that bring you rest?
3. Do you have habits you have incorporated into your day that you can see are actually forms of self-care?
4. What is your current metaphorical oxygen level? Do you think you are operating more from a place of fullness or scarcity?

Invitation to Return

One Minute: God says you are these things: *Chosen. Royal. Holy. Called into His marvelous light. Fearfully and wonderfully made. God's temple, and God's Spirit dwells in you. Loved. A new creation. Healed. Redeemed. An ambassador for Christ. A friend of God. Blessed. The salt of the earth. The light of the world.* Which words stand out to you? Write those words on a piece of paper and place it somewhere in your home you see often. Meditate throughout the week on those words and who you truly are to our Father.

One Hour: Think about your current level of self-care. Jot down some things you do to take care of yourself. What fills your cup? Are you making time for that thing? Now grab your calendar and mark off one hour each week this month for time you will spend intentionally loving yourself. If the budget allows and it's something you enjoy, schedule a massage or a manicure. Plan a coffee date with a friend. Light some candles and soak in the tub with a good book. Whatever it is you love to do. This is your time. Enjoy it!

One Day: Who says you need to stop at one hour? Block off an entire day just for you. It may feel weird, but you are worth it!

PART TWO

RELATIONAL RETURN

There was a man all alone;
he had neither son nor brother.
    There was no end to his toil,
yet his eyes were not content with his wealth.
    "For whom am I toiling," he asked,
"and why am I depriving myself of enjoyment?"
    This too is meaningless—
a miserable business!

Two are better than one,
because they have a good return for their labor:
    If either of them falls down,
one can help the other up.
    But pity anyone who falls
and has no one to help them up.
    Also, if two lie down together, they will keep warm.
But how can one keep warm alone?
    Though one may be overpowered,
two can defend themselves.
    A cord of three strands is not quickly broken.

—Ecclesiastes 4:8–12

6

RETURN TO CONNECTION

Find Holy Ground Right Where You Are

Where does love begin? In our own homes. When does it begin?
When we pray together.

—Mother Teresa, *Everything Starts from Prayer*

One Sunday morning, my husband and I woke early and went outside with coffees in hand. The birds chirped and the cool fall-morning air blew around us. In the quiet, we started to talk about the night before. We had experienced a challenge with one of our teenagers that needed a resolution. This was new territory for us all. We didn't know how to handle it, and the answers weren't coming easily.

Parenting teenagers can feel isolating because the stories are no longer ours to tell. These are our children's stories. And this can be difficult. When they were little, we could get on parenting chat groups and ask questions about potty training and discipline and how to get our kids to eat vegetables without feeling the need to protect their identity. As they got older, we dealt with harder and more personal issues. They needed autonomy, and some of these things they were dealing with needed to land on safe ears and not be exposed to gossip or judgment.

The challenge we faced with our daughter the prior night was one of those situations. While my husband and I dealt with it as best as we knew how, I still found my overanalyzing, overthinking mind reeling that Sunday morning with all the motherhood stresses and what-ifs.

Urgent questions poured from my mouth like water freshly released from a hydrant. Are we doing enough? Are we teaching them enough? Are we instilling the right values in them? Have we focused on what truly matters? How can we make up for what we've missed? What about the bad things we've unintentionally modeled for them? How do we protect them? How do we keep them from the bad things in the world? How can we stay connected as a family as they are growing older and longing for more autonomy? And on and on and on it went.

I was swirling in a giant cloud of tension and anxiety. Even though my husband and I operate as a team, in this moment, I had all six of our futures resting squarely on my shoulders. It was up to me to set things straight. It was up to me to find the answers. It was up to me to train my children in the way they should go.[1] *I better capture this moment. I better get it right.*

And then, right in the middle of that anxiety-storm, an unexpected peace washed over my mind, body, and spirit.

That's how you know peace is from the Lord. It surpasses understanding. God's peace arrives when it is least expected and somehow manages to take you from a ten back down to a one. Or maybe from an eight to a three. Whatever the number, you recognize this peace isn't from some incredible ten-step solution you just dreamed up or from your own strength. No, it happens because of your weakness. When you can't possibly see the end of the panic and the overwhelm, yet the Holy Spirit inside you says, "I've got this. Let it go. Take it off your shoulders and give it to Me." The internal storm settles, and you are reminded once again that when you are weak, God is strong. So you let go. You yoke yourself to Him, and your load is lightened.

This was the kind of peace that settled over my heart. The questions and what-ifs came to a halt. The anxiety I was getting lost in subsided. In that moment of clarity, Patrick and I realized that what we needed was to return to Jesus as a family.

Return to Jesus

Early in our marriage, when our children were very young and things would feel chaotic or I would try to take on the spiritual growth of our family, the questions would pour like they did that early Sunday morning. Only then, I would want a complete overhaul of everything. I would try to answer it all in an instant with a list of things we had to change moving forward. We needed to join a Bible study. We needed to have family meetings every Sunday. We needed to pray every night at bed. We needed accountability partners. And on and on it would go. I would jot down all we needed to accomplish to get back on track. Stat. The only problem was that while these things are all good and my intentions were pure, trying to make many changes all at once meant that nothing stuck. It didn't work for our family.

As my husband and I sat outside with the birds and the breeze, talking about how our family could return to Jesus, we remembered Jesus's words to His disciples: "For where two or three gather in my name, there am I with them."[2]

When we gather as a family to pray, He is with us. When we gather in His name, our attention shifts from the here and now to the eternal. His promises become our anchor as we remember to give Him every request and every praise. When we gather as a family and put Him in the center, we feel His presence and His glory.

We didn't need to make it complicated. We didn't need to devise a grand plan. We needed to pray. To be intentional. To prioritize Jesus and recenter our crazy, harried, busy, stressed-out, and very joyful lives—because there is room for all these emotions—back on the One who longs to give us life in abundance.

Taking a cue from our early days, we knew that if we tried to come up with something grandiose or complicated, the goal would get lost in the shuffle. We might stick with it for a week or two, if we were lucky, but if we tried to add or even change too much, then it wouldn't work. Knowing this, we decided that if daily prayer as a family was going to be a regular part of our lives, then it would need to be a part of a time when we were already together: the dinner table.

Patrick and I have intentionally made mealtime a priority. We gather around the table and take turns sharing about our day and listening to each other—probably better than we do at any other time. Usually, the meal ends with each of us giving a high and a low we experienced that day. These moments often lead to more meaningful conversations and an opportunity to discover how different experiences impact each of us. As the kids have grown, it's been harder for all six of us to be there consistently, but, for the most part, we have committed to sharing a meal and our lives around the table.

The sacred time we longed to build into our schedules was already there waiting for us to put into practice. We decided once a week, preferably on Sunday, we would end the meal not with highs and lows but with praises and prayer requests. Then, we would lift those joys and concerns to the feet of the Maker. As our prayers stretched beyond the blessing of the meal, we would be lifted up and out of our circumstances, and our gazes would be placed back on Jesus.

We knew this would work because we weren't trying to add something extra to our already busy lives. We also knew this would be a time of depth and connection because we saw the power of gathering around the table modeled by Jesus during His time here on Earth.

Jesus often went into the homes of those who loved Him to share a meal. As they gathered to break bread and drink wine, He would tell parables and stories that spoke truth about the Father. He revealed the mystery of who He is in relation to the Father. He spoke truth, wisdom, goodness, and even conviction into the people sitting at the table with Him.

On the night before He died, Jesus shared a meal with His closest companions, even the one whose betrayal would lead to His death:[3]

> As they were eating, Jesus took some bread and blessed it. Then he broke it in pieces and gave it to the disciples, saying, "Take it, for this is my body."
>
> And he took a cup of wine and gave thanks to God for it. He gave it to them, and they all drank from it. And he said to them, "This is my blood, which confirms the covenant between God and his people. It is poured out as a sacrifice for many. I tell you the truth, I will not drink wine again until the day I drink it new in the Kingdom of God."[4]

The broken bread—a symbol of His broken body. The wine—a symbol of the blood He would shed for you and for me and for all of creation that ever would be. A sacred meal shared between God in the flesh and His followers. A meal that echoes through the ages as an invitation to all to join Him at the table.

There is a reason we read often about Jesus gathering in homes to fill His body with food that moved beyond His need for human survival. There is a reason He gathered with His loved ones to share a meal before His time on Earth would come to a brutal end. The table is a place of intimacy. A place where time slows down as we pause for the nourishment of body and soul. It is a place where walls can be broken down. It can be a place where truth is spoken and joy is shared.

When two or more gather in His name, He is there.

So we invite Him to our table. We invite Him to share in our bread and in our wine, and we know He will meet us there with His truth and His love and His grace and all the good gifts He gives. A simple meal becomes holy ground.

This was the answer to our prayer. This was what our family needed.

Time together with Jesus is what we all need, because relationships in life can get out of whack. Do you know what I mean? Have you experienced times when your communication feels a bit off? Times when you are flying by those you love and care for and not truly connecting in the ways you did before?

Maybe you're yelling at the kids or are frustrated with your parents. Maybe you're fighting with a sibling or your spouse. Maybe you're struggling to find common ground with both your immediate and extended family. You can return to Jesus and experience the connection your heart and soul longs for.

When you put God at the center of those relationships, He is with you. He is with your children and your siblings and your parents and your grandparents. Inviting you to experience His peace. Inviting you to unity with those you do life with. With those who are the most precious to you. Inviting you to give Him your burdens, questions, and what-ifs. Inviting you to experience fullness of relationship, not only with Him, but with others, too.

If you are feeling like you could use a spiritual boost in your family, or with another person you are close to, I encourage you to find just one thing. To take one step. To make it applicable to whatever your current situation may be today.

You may be thinking, *Jen, I want to make time for Jesus and my faith, but I'm stretched thin and worn out. And I just don't know how to change or to add anything else to my family's already demanding schedules and lives.*

Friend, I hear you. I couldn't imagine adding one other thing to my six-member household schedule. Instead, we built in the time with another activity—dinner. If you look at your life today, where is there already time built in? Perhaps you have a lengthy car ride in the mornings or afternoons with your children. Could you use that time to pray together? Or maybe you find yourself sitting on the bleachers with your husband at Saturday afternoon games. Could you use that time to do a weekly check-in: "How is your heart? How can I pray for you?" Maybe you and your coworker have lunch together once a week. Could you use that time to ask meaningful questions that engage directly with where they are in their life? Instead of talking about the weather or what you're watching on Netflix, can you show with your words and your questions that you really care about what they are experiencing in the day-to-day?

If you're having trouble finding time in a pre-built activity, then return to Jesus. Give the task to Him in prayer, and trust He will make a way.

When you take an intentional step in your faith to move closer to the Lord and to meet with Him, there will be gifts that come from that step. I am not an absolutes person and try to refrain from the words "never" and "always," but in this moment, I can say that deliberately moving toward God will always produce blessings in your life. Always. And when you move toward God with your loved ones, those blessings will be multiplied.

Jesus in the Mix

As my family shifted our Sunday night highs and lows to praises and prayer requests, we went deeper than the surface of our daily events. Our long conversations and prayers strengthened our connection and intimacy with God and each other.

Think about it: If someone asks how your day was, you are likely to respond with a quick and shallow "fine" or "it was okay." But if someone asks how they can pray for you, you are more likely to share the real and authentic matters of the heart.

The same was true when my family gathered around our table with our struggles and our joys. Our relationships grew in the unique way relationships do when vulnerability is present. As we learned how to talk about the harder things in life and how to pray for each other, our hearts intertwined. As we opened up about our fears and our concerns and the more pressing matters of our days, not just what we had for lunch at school or our worries about an upcoming test, our conversations went longer. They became more authentic. More true. More real.

When you place Jesus at the center of your family, your relationships become fuller. Full of His joy. Full of His peace. Full of His goodness. Full of His faithfulness. Full of His grace. Full of all the gifts of the Spirit. As you move intentionally toward the Lord as a family, you will find a soul satisfaction that is beyond anything the world provides.

You will also learn to really listen to each other. To hear what the other person is going through. As you listen and learn, you may discover that the reason your husband was so snappy this week or your child so disengaged was because of a struggle. Then the question of "How can we pray for you?" becomes an invitation to extend grace. To slow down and see the other person in ways you may otherwise miss as you are running from here to there and back again in your busy week.

You may be in a hard season. In a season of growth and change. In a season when you are feeling the pull and the pressure, and you wake up with your lists, regularly wondering how in the world everything will get done. If you find yourself there right now, know I can very much relate. But I know that these small steps I make with my family, and the small steps you make with your family, are some of the most important steps we will take. I know that finding a way to incorporate these practices and rhythms will have eternal benefits that far outweigh anything else.

And I know the same is true for you and your loved ones, friend. In whatever season you may find yourself, once you discover just one thing to help build intimacy with God and your loved ones, and once you take that step together, you will grow closer.

To God. And to each other.

Of this, I am most definitely certain.

Rhythms of Return

Prayer

Waymaker,

Some seasons are harder than others. I feel the push and the pull and the pain and the pressure, and I want to be with You, but I don't know how. I want to make a way, but I can't seem to figure it out.

Make a way for me, Lord.

Show me those places and spaces I can turn over to You. Help me to take that one intentional step toward You with those I love.

I know time spent with You is the best time spent. I know time spent with those I love is one of the great gifts You have given me. And both of those together are like sweet honey to the lips.

I pray for fullness of relationships. Full of all the gifts of Your Spirit, Lord. I pray they penetrate those places where I gather with those I love. I pray my dinner table becomes a place of holy ground, where hearts are spilling over with Your Love, truth is spoken, pain is mended, growth takes place, and lifelong bonds of closeness with You and with one another are formed.

May I not forget the mission field of my home.

Make a way, Lord.

Help me to take the first small step with my loved ones.

Together.

Amen.

Questions for Reflection

1. What relationships are you struggling with currently? How can you invite Jesus into those relationships?

2. Have you tried things to draw near to Christ as a family in the past? What has worked? What hasn't worked as well? Is there something you notice in particular about the thing or things that have worked? If you have tried to get into spiritual habits with your family or loved ones and they haven't worked, how has that made you feel? Have you felt discouraged? Know it's normal for those things we try to incorporate to not work sometimes, and that's okay—God knows your heart. Keep trying! Different seasons call for different spiritual habits and practices. Remember, there is no "right" answer, and every family is different.

3. Jesus models for us the importance of gathering around the table with loved ones. What has been your experience when you gather around the table with those you love? Have you felt a deeper connection with those you share a meal with? What is it about this experience that resonates, or does not resonate, with you?

4. How can you pray for your loved ones today? Do you need prayer for something specific today? If so, can you make time to ask your loved ones to pray for you? If this isn't something you have done before, it may feel a bit odd, but it could open the door to more deep and meaningful conversations and connection.

Invitation to Return

One Minute: Create a family prayer journal to record prayers and praises from your family. Leave it in a communal spot in the house and encourage everyone to write down prayers and praises throughout the week as they arise. Use this journal and pray either first thing in the morning or at the end of the day before bed. You can choose to pray over every request or, to keep this activity at one minute, place your hand on the journal, pray the Lord's Prayer, and then ask Him to take every request of your family members and hear their prayers.

One Hour: Choose one time per week to gather as a family to pray. Consider times when you are already together and may already be praying. Maybe before bed, on the way to school, or at the dinner table. Make this more intentional than your standard evening or mealtime prayer. Go around and ask for prayer requests and praises. Have someone start and someone else be the closer. Let everyone know they are welcome to pray in the in-between space but will not be forced to. The closer will know that when a time of silence has happened, everyone who wishes to pray has said their prayer and it is time for the prayer to be closed.

One Day: Share a day of praise as a family. Have everyone pick one thing they love to do together and do each of those things. Maybe it's getting ice cream after dinner, playing a family game, or going on a bike ride. After you do each activity, gather in a circle, hold hands, and say a prayer of praise. Acknowledge the gifts God has given your family to make each activity possible. This will not only serve as a reminder to give thanks to the Lord for His gifts but will also grow your family closer. Before you begin, you will want to set some time and monetary parameters to fit everything into one day.

7

RETURN TO REPAIR

Grace Upon Grace Upon Grace

Forgiveness is an act of the will, and the will can function regardless of the temperature of the heart.

—Corrie ten Boom, *The Hiding Place*

My husband, Patrick, and I recently traveled to Indiana to help Shirley, my mother-in-law. Her dementia had been worsening over the past few months, and she needed increased care. My husband and his siblings were trying to find a good home for her and her husband, Clifford, to spend the remainder of their years.

As we pulled up to the house on Friday morning, we saw my brother-in-law on the phone outside. He had just arrived and found their ninety-five-year-old stepfather on the floor with what seemed to be a broken hip and their mom nowhere to be seen. We called an ambulance, and soon after, Shirley walked through the door saying she had gone on a "run." I exchanged a knowing glance with Patrick and my brother-in-law—with Clifford on the ground with a broken hip, there was no question Shirley needed round the clock care, starting now.

We spent the rest of the weekend in my father-in-law's hospital room. The days were mentally, physically, and emotionally draining. This was not the weekend we had imagined, but, thankfully, everyone was going to be as okay as they could be, given the situation.

On Sunday, Patrick drove his mom and stepdad's car and I drove our car home. In the silence, my thoughts rested on Shirley, her husband, Patrick, and Patrick's siblings. I mourned the life Shirley now faced as she slipped deeper into dementia, and I thought, *The next time I see her will probably be worse. Will she forget who I am? And if so, how much longer do we have?* Dementia is a hard condition I hadn't dealt with before. It is unforgiving and incredibly painful to watch as someone you love slowly and consistently slips away. My heart was breaking.

As I grieved, my thoughts shifted to the week ahead. Patrick would be traveling the next morning for work. My cousin was in town and would be staying with me Monday night. My daughter was in the musical *Shrek* for the next two weekends, and I was on the team responsible for feeding the children during rehearsals and on the weekends of the play. And to add to the excitement, that Saturday was also prom, two of our daughters were attending, and we were hosting an after-prom party—*I really should have done a better look over the calendar before I agreed to that one.* And to top it all off, I had pressing deadlines at work.

I created a mental list and worked out the details in my head of how each day had to go for everything to get done. The first order of business was to unpack and clean when I got home so we were ready for my cousin's arrival the next day.

But, as we all know, things don't always go as planned.

My mom had watched the kids while my husband and I were gone. When I got home, she told me that she had maintained the downstairs of our home and left the care of the upstairs to the kids. Sounded incredibly reasonable to me. After all, they were teenagers and perfectly capable of cleaning up after themselves.

When I went upstairs, my jaw dropped. There were clothes on the floor. Old food and drink cups scattered everywhere. Remnants of games and electronic devices casually discarded. It was a teenager's dream and a parent's wreck—not a part of the meticulous plan I had laid out. This was way more cleaning than I had bargained for.

I was not happy.

None of the kids were home, so I sent them texts with picture after picture of each room and a message: "I'm disappointed. We'll talk when you get here."

Not long after, my kids walked in with heads bowed low. Without yelling, I let all the kids know I was upset they hadn't done what was asked of them. During the conversation, I learned one child was much more responsible for the mess than the others, so most of the punishment landed on her shoulders. She rolled her eyes in response, and I fumed internally.

I was depleted. I had just spent the weekend dealing with the unexpected. I was grieving. I was stressed. And now I was angry. She could tell by my tone and eyes that I was hot, and she knew she had pushed it. I dished out her consequence, asked for their devices—they were grounded for the rest of the night—and then sent them upstairs to clean. All without raising my voice. Message delivered. I was proud of my level-headed parenting and gave myself a mental congratulatory pat on the back. I handled it well.

But really, I didn't. Because I didn't move on. I continued to silently fume around the house as I aggressively wiped down counters, vacuumed, and mopped. Even though I wasn't yelling, she could feel it. And sometimes, it's the silent anger that can hurt the most.

I didn't realize the pain I was causing her until later that night. As my husband and I were tucking her in and saying good night, he noticed she looked sad.

Patrick told her, "We were angry, but we've moved on. We aren't thinking about what happened anymore. We have forgiven you."

Her eyes shifted and locked onto mine, and I knew what she already knew in her heart—I hadn't really forgiven her.

I was holding on to my anger. What she did wasn't really that bad. But my own personal issues and agenda for the evening had been inconvenienced by her literal mess. I hadn't accepted her apology, given her grace, or forgiven her. I hadn't moved on.

Ouch. His words landed hard.

When Patrick left the room, I asked my daughter if I could climb into bed with her and hold her for a bit. Even though she is a teenager, I still snuggle as often as any of my children will let me. She nodded. I climbed in, wrapped my arms around her, and she immediately started crying.

I whispered in her ear, "I love you. I forgive you. No matter what you do, my love for you will never change."

We hugged until her tears stopped falling. Then she told me she had written me a letter before climbing into bed. She handed me the letter, we said good night, then I left to read it.

In her note, she said how sorry she was and that she understood if I could not forgive her. My heart dropped. How could she think I wouldn't forgive her? Then I thought of my internal fuming. My insides had spilled out into the space around us—and she knew. Until that moment in bed, I hadn't forgiven her. I hadn't shown her any grace. I hadn't hugged her and told her how much I loved her. I hadn't asked her about her weekend and how she spent her time while we were away. I hadn't told her anything about our trip to Fort Wayne. I was lingering on her past mistakes and how they were inconveniencing me at that time. I hadn't moved forward.

She cried when I climbed into bed because she was worried I would not be able to let this thing go—this silly thing. This thing of little consequence. This thing I made bigger than I probably needed to.

I put her letter down, went upstairs, and told her, "I will always forgive you. Just as you forgive me, just as God forgives us. I'm sorry for the way I responded." We hugged again. We prayed. She forgave me. More I-love-yous were said. Then, with gratitude in my heart and my arms wrapped snug around her, I let go of my anger and frustration. She let go of her guilt and shame. We moved forward.

When my daughter chose not to do as she had been asked, to take care of our home, she created a tear in our relationship. When I chose to internally fume, I widened that distance. But we walked through a cycle of repair—apologies, forgiveness, and grace—to fix the damage we had created. My daughter started the cycle when she recognized her mistake, apologized, and sought forgiveness. And, although it took longer than it probably should have, when I accepted her apology, forgave her, and apologized for my actions, I added more stitches to the tear. Then, as I climbed into my daughter's bed, wrapped my arms around her, and told her how much I loved her, we closed the cycle together through extended grace—no matter what happened, we still loved each other, we still forgave each other, and we chose to repair the damage we had created. Even after the hurt we caused one another in our moments of selfishness. That is the beauty of grace. In the wake of hurt, trust and love still persevere.

This was not the first time I have entered this cycle with my daughter, and it will not be the last. But every time we mend a tear, the fabric of our relationship gets stronger. With every "I'm sorry" and "I forgive you," she and I lean into unconditional love and grow in trust that no matter what happens, the well of grace will not run dry.

There is a wooden sign I made for our home shortly after we

moved to Tennessee. It hangs over our front door with a simple message that packs a profound punch: "Grace upon grace upon grace." I knew I needed this sign and that it would probably be a good message for anyone coming in and out of our home, really, because we all need grace.

We know we will mess up, and we want to know there is enough grace to cover it all. To know that we are still loved, still accepted, still forgiven, no matter what we do. There isn't a moment when we think, *Okay, that's enough grace for me today.* No, on the contrary: we long for that kind of wraparound grace. We need it all day, every day, and we need to learn to give it, just as it's given to us.

Return to Jesus

Jesus offers His children a never-ending well of grace to dip our hands into and drink from. A chance to let His grace flow through us and from us. A way for our relationships to be washed by grace. And an opportunity to model for others what the love, redemption, and grace of Christ look like in action.

Jesus came to this world to be the bridge between God and us. He willingly walked the Via Dolorosa—the Way of Suffering—to repair our relationship to God.[1] The weight of our sin and pain and heartache and tribulation and death and sorrow fell on Him and mixed with the real human pain He was experiencing. Yet Jesus didn't curse us. He didn't focus on all the ways we wronged Him. He didn't blow up the Earth and say, "That's it. They are beyond hope." He said, "Father, forgive them, for they do not know what they are doing."[2]

In excruciating pain, His response was, and is, "Father, forgive them." When God as man took His final breath, His thoughts were on us. On reconciling us to Him. On giving us *grace*.

The wages for our sin is death, but we are offered life to the full.[3]

Jesus became sin on our behalf.[4] He took our sins on His innocent shoulders and became the sacrificial lamb for us. Payment made. We are free. We deserve death, but we are given life through Christ. This is what true grace looks like.

This gift of grace is free, but how can that be? The idea of a free gift is something we have been taught to be leery of and to not accept without looking at all the angles the giver may be coming from. We are taught that if it's too good to be true, it probably is. We also may draw from life experiences where those we love gave to us with strings attached. Maybe we don't have a lot of experience in our personal lives with this notion of an unmerited gift we aren't able to earn or lose. Maybe this notion of something for free with no price to be paid is completely counter to what we've experienced up until now. Yet this is what Jesus gives us.

And grace is there for all of us to both receive and give. We apologize. We forgive. We open our hands to the gift of grace. We return to Jesus and see the depth to which we are forgiven. And then we, in turn, give that gift of forgiveness to others. We are forgiven for much and we long to forgive for much.

Grace upon grace upon grace.

Recognize the Cycle

As we return to Jesus and our eyes open to this daily, unending gift, we begin to see the cycle—repentance of our wrongs, forgiveness, and acceptance of grace—as a welcomed path toward our healing, reconciliation, and peace with others.

There are so many times and ways I mess up in a day. I snap at my husband and children. I become self-absorbed and self-focused and don't lift my head to even acknowledge the person who is right next to me. I am impatient when I'm driving and start to ride the bumper of the car in front of me—hoping they will get the message. I listen to music or watch shows that may not be the best for me. I drink one too many glasses of wine or eat one too many cookies before bed to try to numb out after a hard day. The list goes on and on . . .

But in every instance, I am never left alone. Jesus is always right there. Waiting for me to see the invitation to return to Him. To acknowledge my wrong, to hand it to Him, to ask Him for forgiveness and move forward in His grace. In not just the big things, but in the small things as well. Sometimes, I feel that gentle nudge from the Holy Spirit and am quick to notice the error of my ways and give it to Him, and other times, it may take me days before I realize I could have handled that situation a little better than I did.

With my daughter, I was so blinded by the wrong that someone else had done to me that I missed the wrong in my actions. I focused on the mess my kids made while I was away. I focused on the eye-rolling and the lack of respect shown in a moment of disobedience. What I couldn't see was the pain I was causing as I stormed around the house, refusing to let go.

Have you been there? Has all your internal fuming caused you to heap burning mental coals on the person who has done you wrong—without ever taking a second to consider what you may have done to contribute to the relational problem you find yourself in? Have you ruminated on something someone else said or did? Replaying the conversation over and over in your mind of how you are going to address all the harm they caused you, without asking yourself if there is something you need to clean up on your side of the street first? Have you gone into a conversation prepared to attack, with all your mental come-backs ready, instead of walking into the conversation ready to begin with your own apology? Has your anger, frustration, or even judgment of someone else during a conflict made it hard to move forward?

You can't enter the cycle of repair when you are blind to your own wrongs in the situation. So Jesus gently whispers in your ear:

> Why do you look at the speck of sawdust in your brother's eye and pay no attention to the plank in your own eye? How can you say to your brother, "Let me take the speck out of your eye," when all the time there is a plank in your own eye? You hypocrite, first take the plank out of your own eye, and then you will see clearly to remove the speck from your brother's eye.[5]

When we're stuck looking at the wrongs done to us, Jesus powerfully reminds us to always be aware of our own actions. Our own words. Our own sin. Instead of pointing fingers and yelling, "Look at what you've done! Look at how wrong you are!" we need to pause and ask ourselves, or better yet, ask God, "What is my role in this? How have I contributed? What do I need to acknowledge in my own life? Is there something I need to repent of in this moment—to both God above and the loved one I have harmed?"

By focusing on our own plank, our hearts are softened and our eyes are opened. Suddenly, we aren't quite as angry about that speck of sawdust because we see the log and know the grace we need in that moment. We become remorseful and more full of grace for others. We are moved to own the times we sin, not just against the Lord but also against each other. We recognize we've hurt someone else, and we humble ourselves before them.

Admitting our wrongs and apologizing take the relationship so much further than moving on and pretending nothing ever happened. When we acknowledge the pain we caused someone, we are laying it before them, and we are, in many ways, saying, "I see this hurt I caused you, and my heart hurts for it. I will try not to do this to you again."

Here is where the relief of forgiveness steps in. When the one you wronged sees your heart and says, "I see you. I see your remorse and know your heart. I trust you to not hurt me in the same way again," then you can breathe. Their words become a healing balm to the relationship because you are seen, you are known, you are loved, you are forgiven. Through forgiveness, grace begins the work of covering and mending and healing.

Admitting when you're wrong isn't always easy. Asking for forgiveness isn't always easy, and sometimes, accepting grace isn't easy, either. But when you enter these spaces and allow the cycle of repair to penetrate your relationship in a moment of hurt and wounding, your relationship will grow.

Think of the relationships where you have had to go to the hard spaces, admit your wrongs, ask for forgiveness, and then accept that you have been forgiven. There is something special and unique about those relationships, isn't there? There is a depth that occurs when you go through this cycle with others.

But, Jen, what if I can't move forward? What if I can't go through this cycle with someone?

Friend, in a perfect world free from sin and pain, all relationships would move forward in perfect love and unity with our Lord and one another, but we don't live in a perfect world. We live in a world with suffering, abuse, neglect, trauma, and a myriad of other relationship destroyers. And while the goal, and hope, is reconciliation, I recognize that this is not always the reality.

Some relationships are not meant to last, especially if there is abuse of any kind. If you find yourself in a relationship that has moved into the toxic realm, please know it is not only good, but sometimes very necessary for your own well-being, to walk away. Sometimes, the wisest thing we can do is leave.

You can enter the repair cycle and still decide you cannot move forward with the relationship. You can forgive someone and create healthy boundaries to avoid toxic situations in the future. You can apologize for your wrong, clean up your side of the street, hopefully reconcile, and say goodbye.

Saying goodbye probably won't be easy. It probably will hurt—maybe for a long, long time. But sometimes, the repair cycle doesn't end in continued relationship. Sometimes the cycle stops at the forgiveness and then a parting of ways so both sides can find health and healing separately.

I'm sorry if you are in that spot, friend. I'm sorry if you are in the midst of ending a relationship with one you held dear. It's not easy, but sometimes, it's the best option to protect yourself and heal. You'll know the direction to go when you seek guidance from the One who heals, protects, and redeems.

Accept Jesus's invitation to return. Bow at His feet and ask for courage to walk the cycle of repair. To say, "I am sorry." To be humble enough to admit when you are wrong. To seek and offer forgiveness. To lay that thing down and not pick it up again. To create healthy boundaries. To move forward, trusting Him with each step you take.

Rhythms of Return

Prayer

Builder of Bridges,

Thank You for the well of grace I can dip my hands into and drink from fully for all of eternity. Thank You for the well of grace that flows through me and from me as it spills into the relationships with those I encounter each and every day.

May I learn to repent of those things I need to repent of. To acknowledge my wrongs and to look others fully in the eye and say, "I am sorry for the pain I caused. Will you forgive me?"

When I am weak, You are strong.

Be my strength, Lord.

And when I can no longer move forward, give me the wisdom and courage to walk away.

Thank You for relational healing.

Thank You for the gift of grace poured out on the cross.

Thank You for mending the torn fabric in my relationships.

Thank You for being the stitching that makes the fabric stronger.

You are the redeemer of relationships.

Let me not forget it.

Amen.

Questions for Reflection

1. When have you seen the cycle of repair—repentance, forgiveness, and grace—play out clearly in a relationship? What stands out to you about that time? Did this help you to grow closer to this person?

2. Is there someone you need to apologize to today to begin the cycle of repair? What would that look like for you to begin to make amends and move forward in this cycle?

3. Have you had a relationship end due to unhealthy patterns? Have you taken time to grieve that loss? How do you feel about that relationship now? Do you feel you have fully forgiven them?

4. Think of a relationship that you consider to be very healthy. What is it about that relationship that makes it that way? What stands out to you? Thank God for the gift of that relationship today.

Invitation to Return

One Minute: We all make mistakes. It is inevitable. Those in our lives will make mistakes. It is inevitable. At the end of the day, before your head hits the pillow, kneel by your bedside and ask God to show you areas throughout the day where you need His forgiveness, and ask Him for that forgiveness.

One Hour: Go back to question three. If you are ready, begin the cycle of repair by reaching out to the person. Schedule a time to meet or talk so that you can acknowledge your plank, offer your apology, and begin to move forward in a healthy relationship. If you do not have anyone in mind, then use this time for meditation, prayer, and journaling. Play some music. Think on your relationships, on the grace given and grace received, and thank God for the gift of repair that has happened in your life.

One Day: Is there someone you recently went through the cycle of repair with? Celebrate that relationship and schedule a day to have fun together this week.

8

RETURN TO WISDOM

It's Okay to Say No

Saying no isn't an unnecessary rejection. It's a necessary protection of our Best Yes answers.

—Lysa TerKeurst, *The Best Yes*

During the pandemic, life slowed down tremendously for our family. In many ways, we were privileged, because our experience differed from those who were at the front lines in medical facilities, who were sick, or who tragically lost loved ones. Yet our time wasn't without its challenges. Our children learned online for a year, spent very little time engaging with peers, and couldn't participate in extracurriculars they once enjoyed. While the pandemic was hard, I can see the many gifts wrapped up in that time, especially learning to rest together.

With the kids learning from home and my husband now working from home, we spent weeks in both the fall and winter at our favorite location: a red, wooden family cottage on Walloon, Lake Michigan. Its wraparound screened porch, large brick fireplace, and old hardwood floors exuded warmth. The house was full of nostalgia and held a wall marked with the height of every family member to ever have walked through the doors, and furniture hand-painted by my grandmother. And the pandemic allotted us time to slow down and make lifelong memories in this century-old home.

We returned to the basics. We spent time in nature. We cooked meals together and lingered at the long wooden table on the seat cushions my grandmother needlepointed for each of her children. We buried our noses in books, pieced together puzzles, and played Monopoly for two straight days. We picked up new hobbies and skills—like baking homemade rolls, cookies, and deep-dish pizzas; frying chicken in the skillet; playing piano; and crocheting brightly colored tops. Skills that will hopefully last a lifetime. We could do these things because there was nowhere to go and nothing that had to be done. In the stillness, I saw the importance of space and rest for my family's spiritual, mental, and physical well-being.

When life resumed as usual, I struggled with the hurried pace we were jumping back into. We went from a hundred to zero and back to a hundred, and I was growing increasingly frustrated with its speed. I felt like we hadn't learned a thing from that time off. In some ways, we seemed more committed than ever to doing all the things and accepting all the invitations that came our way.

Maybe we were trying to make up for lost time?

I don't know.

But what I do know is: it just wasn't working for us.

I got cranky.

My husband got cranky.

The kids got cranky.

And even the cats got cranky, because we weren't respecting their need for consistent nap and meal schedules. (Really, we can learn a lot from the cats.)

The crankier we all became, the worse our home life became. Everyone was irritable, self-absorbed, and impatient. We snapped at each other for reasons that, if we were well rested and cared for, we probably wouldn't care so much about. We were overbooked, stretched thin, and in desperate need of some rest.

I had known some semblance of pre-pandemic life was necessary, but I didn't want *this*. *Please, Lord*, I begged. *I don't want to go back to this stressed-out routine.*

But what could we do? This was the world we lived in. We couldn't stop it. We couldn't resist it.

Or could we?

Return to Jesus

For the past few weeks, we have been watching the multi-season series *The Chosen* together as a family.[1] There is so much I love about the show, but one thing that has really stood out is the practice of the Sabbath. I love how they portray the importance of this meal as part of Jewish tradition and worship of God. But I am especially drawn to, and intrigued by, the number of times they greet each other with the words *Shabbat shalom*.

Shabbat shalom means sabbath of peace,[2] or peaceful rest, and is a phrase used to greet friends and family, or to bid them farewell, on the Jewish Sabbath and the days leading up to it. The tradition honors God's rest on the seventh day of creation and His instruction for us to take a day of rest each week.[3] Sacred rest.

Could you imagine what it would be like if our families encouraged Shabbat shalom? If, instead of rushing past each other, we paused, looked each other in the eyes, and said words encouraging peaceful rest? There is power in that image. Because the Maker of the heavens and the earth and all of creation has breathed that deep need within each of our souls for sacred rest.

While we are not bound by the same Old Testament laws as the Israelites once were, and we don't need to practice the Sabbath in a legalistic sense,[4] we can see once again that God gives us instruction not to make our lives more difficult but to help us live abundantly. He knows the importance of taking time off from our busy schedules to simply be.

During His ministry, Jesus modeled the importance of this holy rest. He took time to be still and to be apart from the crowds. But he also encouraged His followers to participate in rest. In Mark, Jesus sent His disciples into the world to teach, cast out demons, and heal the sick by themselves. Can you imagine what that must have been like? Did they question whether they had what it takes to do what Jesus asked? And when they were teaching, rebuking, and healing, how much pain and how many pleading eyes did the disciples see? How heartbroken were they for the people surrounding them? Can you imagine the faith and great emotional and physical stamina they needed?

When they finally returned, His disciples were probably *exhausted*. They told Jesus everything they had done and taught, but at some point either before, during, or after they finished telling Jesus all these things, their group encountered such a large number of people coming and going that they couldn't even break to eat. And we all know what happens when we are exhausted and hungry. Hello, hangry.

Jesus saw their need and essentially said no to the people surrounding them. He told His disciples, "'Come with me by yourselves to a quiet place and get some rest.' So they went away by themselves in a boat to a solitary place."[5]

Jesus prioritized rest for His companions. He prioritized intimacy. Now, I'm not sure how long it took to get to their destination, but in that time, the disciples were alone with Jesus. They spent time with Him and were refreshed by His presence. Perhaps they even grew closer as a group. The text is sparse, but we do know that when they landed on the other side of the sea, they engaged with *over five thousand people*. (Can you imagine? My introvert side just shuddered.)

Jesus saw His disciples were weary and burned out after just returning from a grueling time. I bet He also saw those thousands of people coming and knew His disciples needed to recover and refill. So He invited them to rest with Him.

I wanted to create that same kind of rest with my family, like the days we spent at the cottage. Space to do nothing. Space to lounge and play puzzles. Space to let Jesus fill our cups.

In her book *The Best Yes: Making Wise Decisions in the Midst of Endless Demands,* author Lysa TerKeurst says, "Our decisions aren't just isolated choices. Our decisions point our lives in the directions we're about to head. Show me a decision and I'll show you a direction."[6]

Our decisions aren't made in a vacuum. They affect our lives and the lives of our loved ones. The way we choose to spend our time does matter, and it's important we learn to respect and treasure our time. Not just for our sake, but also for the sake of those we love.

Before the pandemic, my family and I were running on fumes. Post-pandemic, we found ourselves back in that fumy state of exhaustion because of our choices and commitments. We had willingly said yes to so many things and were now trying to survive on the fast lane.

Have you experienced this breakneck speed with little to no rest because of your decisions? Perhaps you've said yes to every project at work so you could prove your worth and move up in the company. Or maybe you know the hurried life of youth sports, academic achievements, and every other activity a child participates in. Or maybe your travel schedule is a nonstop flight to the land of jetlag, pushing the limits of sleep and becoming an obstacle to your time with family. Regardless of where you are on the fast track, we weren't meant to live at this speed. I feel that truth deep in my bones.

Like the disciples, we are overwhelmed, burned out, and hangry, but Jesus invites us to rest together with Him. When we silence the demands of the week and spend time with Jesus and our families, then we experience the same restoration and growth as the disciples. There is no question. This is what Jesus does.

You may notice the changes gradually. Maybe you are slower to anger and less likely to lash out. Maybe your husband becomes more aware of his stressors, hands them to Jesus, and is faster to walk in the way of His light and truth. Instead of responding in frustration because the game he's watching is interrupted by someone asking him to take out the trash, he may become more aware of the needs of those around him and quicker to move from annoyance to service. Maybe your teenager isn't as quick to respond with an eyeroll, an exasperated sigh, or a mumble under the breath as a response to what you thought was really a simple question. When the noise is silenced and our thoughts move from the temporal to the eternal, our lives will be transformed.

We want this life-giving, world-changing fruit, but we easily get caught up in the hamster wheel of life. Running, running, running, and wondering, *What in the world am I doing all this running for? What fruit is all this running producing?* We want depth and to be focused on those things that truly matter with those we love, *but how?*

How do we find the balance of our *yes* replies and our *no* replies when life is pulling us in a million directions? How do we commit to making sacred space in our schedules when there are so many needs to be met?

We learn to say no.

Friend, this was a hard lesson for me. I'm a people-pleaser

and a helper; saying no doesn't come naturally. Whenever I saw an open space in our calendar, I wanted to fill it. I wanted to say yes to everyone and everything. But I had to learn discernment. Because when I said yes to something, I was saying no to something else, and that no was usually to rest for my family.

I learned that saying no—even to the good things—was okay. Boundaries were healthy. Even if there was nothing else on the calendar, "no" was a completely acceptable answer. I didn't need to explain my reason to anyone else. I could just decline an invitation. "No" was a full sentence.

You don't have to explain, either. When your family needs rest, you don't need to come up with some kind of excuse as to why the party or Bible study or baseball game won't work for you. You can just say no. Or, if that feels a little rude or abrupt, try, "Thank you for the invitation, but that isn't going to work for us." Period.

Saying no isn't always easy. Sometimes it's downright hard. But sometimes it's the right word to protect your well-being. And those who love you will understand. They will want what is best for you. Just as you do for them.

What if, by adopting this practice of saying no, you learn that you are not controlled by your schedule, but rather that your schedule is something you control? Yes, there is work and school and certain things that must be done during the week, but much of what you do is a choice, even if it doesn't always feel that way. You have the power to say yes or no to everything on your calendar. And as it is with most things in life, the more you practice, the easier saying no will become.

If you find yourself in a place where your schedule has gotten the better of you, then you can course correct. You can reevaluate those things you have said yes to and, if necessary, you can decide to let go of those things. To everything there is a season, and I know sometimes I hold on to things past their point of expiration simply because I have grown comfortable or I have forgotten how to say no. Maybe the same is true for you?

There may even come time for some of the good things in life to go. Bible studies, small groups, and acts of service are all fruitful things you have been called to, but it's important to always go back to your *why*. Why are you doing this? Does it still work for this season? Is this something you are being called to now, or is it time to lay this down?

When life is feeling chaotic and these questions surface, it's time to set your schedule at the feet of the Lord. Pray about what to keep and what to hand over. Talk to your family about what you are doing and what needs to change. Then listen. What does your family need? Now? In this season? What can you incorporate into your lives that will actually build strength of character, deepen faith, and create stronger connections between you and those around you? Then look for little ways—not the big, month-long vacation ways—to incorporate those things into your schedule.

Sometimes we erroneously believe rest can only come during those designated times we reserve for "vacation." During these calculated breaks, we allow ourselves to do the things that slow us down and restore our souls. We maybe pick up that book we've been wanting to read, take a nap on the hammock, or spend extra time in the Word and journaling. Our brains and bodies have been taught that we've reserved vacation for rest, but we need to train our brains and bodies to know that other time is available for a reprieve from the grind.

What if you come to see these times of saying no as mini vacations built into your week? What incredible possibilities lie waiting when you haven't penciled in every waking minute of your days? What would your eyes be open to in your life? How would that impact your relationship with God and others? Wouldn't you love to find out?

Practicing Rest

As I said before, this season has been hard, and it's also one of the busiest I can remember. All four of our children are very active, my husband is traveling almost weekly, and I am working more than I have in years; but even with all the excitement each day can hold, I am also experiencing more peace than I have in quite some time. I believe one of the reasons for this peace is the aerial view I've adopted of our schedules.

Instead of looking at each day on the calendar individually, I look at the days collectively and consider the big picture when making decisions. If we have something on most days and nights of the week and Saturday is wide open, then I leave Saturday open. That doesn't mean we can't hang out with friends or family or do something fun on that day. Instead, it leaves room for us to check in with each other and ask how we are feeling. Do we need extra rest because of the busy week we just had? Or would we like to grab a bite to eat with some friends? Because the day is clear, we can adjust our plans based on where we are mentally, physically, or emotionally.

During these days off, our family discovers space to replenish our souls. We fill our tanks. We've found a way to slow down and be more present with one another. And though the space to rest is welcomed, there is an extra layer of fun and spontaneity that's fulfilling and exciting. Anything can happen.

The pre-planned stillness and quiet also creates ways for us to connect with God. My daughter hits the ivory keys of the piano and worship music fills our home—we connect with God. We go on a family walk through the woods and surround ourselves with nature—we connect with God. We say prayers around the table and dig into the Nashville hot chicken my daughter learned to make—we connect with God. We set aside the distractions and stress and refocus on the things that matter—we connect with God.

To keep this pace, I pray over our calendar and invitations when they come my way. I don't always remember to do this, but when I do, I know it helps because the choices I am making are being filtered through the lens of my faith. And then I permanently schedule non-scheduled days into our calendars—ironic, right? But it works for me. If the month ahead looks particularly crazy, I mark off days of nothing for our family. When I see "no plans" on the calendar, even though I may be tempted to accept an invitation or reach out to friends and make plans, I don't. Because I remember the *why* of preserving this sacred time.

I remember that carving out time for rest and togetherness with our Lord and each other fills our cups. I remember that teaching our children the importance of sacred space will keep them connected to the sacred things of life. I remember that we are modeling healthy boundaries when we say no, and our children will carry that practice into their future. So even when other invitations come our way, I remember our *why* and commit to keeping this space for our family.

What are your reasons for reserving space for your family? Are you longing to know and understand the members of your family better? To know what makes them tick and what the true desires of their hearts may be? Are you wanting a moment to simply be together in a time when it feels like just gathering for dinner is a small miracle? Do you desire time with your parents or grandparents but keep putting off that meal you want to invite them to? Do you see a family member who is struggling and want to speak to them about the love Jesus has for them? All our reasons are different but worth paying attention to. Your reason will point you back to the desires of your heart. To those things that truly matter to you. Find your reason and make that your priority.

As you think about your own schedule, remember to return to Jesus. Take your calendar to Him and ask for guidance. What activities or commitments are no longer serving you well? Should you say yes or no to hosting the after-prom parties? Should you commit to weekly Bible studies in your house? What day(s) should you block off to rest? Should you block off a day to rest each week?

Maybe scheduling days without plans won't work for your family in this season, and that's okay. But perhaps God is calling you to take a weekend off, or even an entire week. Maybe He's leading you to take a staycation without a single plan in place and is waiting to show you what each day holds. Can you imagine the grand adventure that would await you when you woke?

When you hand your schedule to God, you will start to live into the rest He offers you. And the more you live into it, the more you will long for it in your days. The more you will seek out sacred time with your loved ones. The more you will be intentional together in carving out that space of rest and stillness with either plans or no plans. The more you long for it, the easier making time and protecting that time becomes. Because you learn that resting in Him together is where relationships grow.

Shabbat shalom.

Rhythms of Return

Prayer

Sacred One,

I am busy. I am distracted. I am pulled. I am running, running, running on the hamster wheel of my life. But I want to be present. Available. Growing and living and breathing and resting together in the most loving and connected of ways.

So I give You my years, months, days, and hours. Order my steps and help me to make decisions that are good for me and for those I love. Help me to see what needs to go on my calendar, and what needs to remain off.

Father, I pray for a spirit of wisdom, discernment, and revelation so that I can clearly see the invitations I need to decline. Remind me that for everything there is a season.

Just because something is "no" for now doesn't mean it has to be "no" forever. Sometimes, it's just "not yet."

Help me to return my schedule to You, Lord. Thank You for Your faithfulness and goodness, and for modeling for me what it looks like to spend time with You in stillness, in silence, and in peace.

May I grow in depth of relationship with my family and loved ones as we return to You and rest with You. May we find contentment and peace and solace and comfort in those things that matter.

With You at the center. Always at the center of it all.
Peaceful rest.
Shabbat shalom.
Amen.

Questions for Reflection

1. What is your current schedule like? Do you feel stressed or like there is no room for relaxation?
2. If you answered yes to the question above, what would it look like for you to create margin? Does this even seem possible? If it seems impossible, why is that?
3. When is a time you felt like you had more margin? What about that time stands out? Do you feel you experienced personal, relational, and spiritual growth during that time?
4. What are your reasons for reserving space for your family? What are some of your goals or fruit you would like to see come from this time of reserved rest?

Invitation to Return

One Minute: Pray over your calendar. Pray for wisdom and discernment when making plans, and ask the Lord to show you if there is one thing you can get rid of this week to create space.

One Hour: For thirty minutes, do something with your family that will bring fruit to your day. Then write in a journal about that experience. Or, if you would rather, do something for an entire hour with your family that will fill your cups. Be present in the moment with them, and afterward, talk about how you felt after taking time off from the grind and doing something intentional and fun to-gether.

One Day: Consider having at least one day a month—or week, if possible—for a "No Plans Day" with your fam-ily. Protect and preserve this space, knowing that it will leave you breathing room as well as room for spontaneity—which are both wonderful things.

9

RETURN TO COMMUNITY

An Invitation to Friendship

A day without a friend is like a pot without a single drop of honey left inside.

—A. A. Milne, *Winnie-the-Pooh*

I get lost in myself sometimes. With a plethora of things pulling me in an infinite number of directions throughout the day, I can get absorbed in my tasks. I wash, dry, and fold laundry. I pay bills. I drive the kids from here to there and back again. I check emails and meet deadlines. I make doctor and dentist appointments. I buy groceries and make meals. I clean the house. And on and on it goes . . .

I get so wrapped up in the demands of my life that I forget to pause and look up to see all that's happening in the world around me.

In some ways, this self-focused lifestyle has been modeled by our culture. In the United States, we pride ourselves on our independence. Most of us don't live in villages or communities where we rely heavily on each member to work for the greater good of the whole. We no longer work on a barter system where we are trading goods and services. We don't need to share our skills with one another to ensure our survival. Contrary to this communal lifestyle that still exists in some parts of the world, Americans are, for the most part, independent.

We rise in the morning, get ready, and head out the door to work (or quite possibly, since the pandemic, to the office in our home with our business shirt on the top and our pajamas on the bottom). We pick up the kids from school, run our errands, and then pull quickly back into our garage with the door promptly shutting behind us.

We might wave to our neighbor or engage in some idle chit-chat about the weather or the kids. But, for most of us, that is the extent of our interactions with those around us. I'm not saying this to cause shame or create guilt. This is just the way it is for many. We don't spend a lot of time looking outside of ourselves because we don't have to. But when we stay in our bubbles of independence, we miss out on so much because we are meant to be in relationship with others.

God is relational. He in and of Himself is not one, but three. He is the Father, the Son, and the Holy Spirit. He is three parts all residing together since the beginning of time for all of eternity, bringing redemption to the world. All parts necessary for the whole, working for His glory and His good. And we are created in His image. We, too, are relational.

From the very beginning, we see we were made for relationship. When God created Adam, He saw it wasn't good for him to be alone, so God created Eve. Humans weren't designed to live a life of isolation, but rather a life in community with the Lord and with those around us—our friends, family, neighbors, co-workers. Whether we gather around a table to share a meal, worship together on Sunday morning, join a neighborhood book club, volunteer at the school, or meet with a friend for coffee, goodness happens.

When I spend time with people who really know me and get me, with people who love me as I am, with people who have seen me in my highs and my lows and all the in-betweens, with people who don't expect me to fulfill something that was never mine to fulfill, with people who I know will pray for me—and with me—my heart and soul are fed in a unique way. I can breathe a big sigh of relief in their presence, kick off my shoes, look them in the eye and say whatever it is that comes to mind with confidence that they won't judge me or my unwashed hair. They won't try to fix me; they will just love.

But getting to that level of depth and understanding with others doesn't just happen overnight. Friendships take time and effort, a willingness to share your heart and your story and to listen to the hearts and stories of others, too.

To my dear introverted friend who probably just cringed a little: you, too, need friendship with others. Before you close this book, hear me. I know too many people can be draining, but you don't need to be with a ton of people to experience meaningful connection. Having just one person you rely on can make all the difference. And that is good.

On the flip side, to my extroverted friend: you may live your life with a "the more the merrier" mentality. You may amass friends everywhere you go, but that doesn't mean you can't create deep connections. That just means that you may be more willing to accept the invitations that come your way. You may jump at every chance you get for coffee or a backyard barbecue. You may have a harder time creating space with that social calendar of yours, but that's okay. You will figure out your *yes* and your *no* replies, and you will make meaningful connections in those spaces you travel. That, too, is good.

Because wherever you stand on the social spectrum, you aren't made to be alone. You aren't made to be isolated. You are made to be with others. Once you have a taste of true community and deep friendship with someone else who loves you with no strings attached, then your life will be changed.

But maybe you've built a wall around your heart because of old wounds? Maybe you have loved and lost and have vowed to never love and lose again. Or maybe you feel like you just don't have the energy or the mental capacity to deal with relationships. After all, with all the demands pressing in, who even has time in the day for friends?

Or maybe you hear all this and something stirs inside you. A longing wells up because you do want friends in your life, but then you stop and ask yourself, "How do I even go about making a friend at this stage when I can barely even make time to do the things I need to do in a given day?"

How?

Return to Jesus

The chips and queso I usually couldn't wait to dig into had lost their luster. The lump in my throat made it hard to swallow food. Was anyone else feeling how hard it was to breathe?

Minutes before dinner, Patrick told me that his office would be relocating to Nashville, Tennessee, in three years. We had just over two years to make the decision on whether he would stay with that company or leave. Who could live in that space of indecision and waiting for so long? What they were asking of us felt impossible. I was fuming.

With all four kids gathered around the table, we talked in hushed tones and code. They didn't need to know this. I could barely handle it myself. It was the last thing they needed to preoccupy their little minds. No, their minds needed to remain on the tiny Shopkins toys that littered my house and on hurrying home to play outside with the neighborhood kids, not on a move that would upend life as they knew it.

All I could think in that moment was about the friends we

had made while living in Indiana. We were involved in our church community, had close bonds with our neighbors, and had developed some of the deepest and most authentic friendships we had ever experienced. I believed we were in our forever home, in our forever community, and what we had developed in the space where we resided was so very, very good.

I felt a fear bubble in my heart. It had taken so many years. So many Bible studies. So many dinners. So many walks and coffees and bonfires and playdates and deep belly laughs and uncontrollable tears falling in moments of total vulnerability. How could we just walk away from all this beauty and connection?

How would we ever find this again?

I was angry. I was scared. I feared losing what we had. I was worried we would never find it again. I turned to my husband and whispered, "If we decide to go, then I won't speak to you for a year. I'll go if that's what is necessary and, eventually, I'll be okay, but your penance for uprooting me from my forever home will be one year of silence." It's hard to accept now that I said that, but I did. And as ridiculous as it sounds, at that time, I believed it to be true.

But it's amazing how God works. How he can tenderly replace our heart of stone with something softer and more pliable. You see, that impossible time span of three years was exactly the amount of time I needed to move from a stance of fear to possibility and, dare I say, excitement at the idea of a new adventure for our family.

I knew we would miss our friends. I knew that those companions could never be replaced, because they are unique and irreplaceable. But God reminded me that just like my heart expanded and grew with each baby placed in my arms, my heart would expand and grow in our new place of residence.

I wasn't losing those bonds forever. I was just adding more, and God revealed how I could find those new relationships through the life of Jesus and His companions.

One of the first things Jesus did when His ministry began was to gather His followers—His friends. He spent intentional time traversing the land to find His people. And when He found them, Jesus called out to them.

Each disciple didn't say "I am too busy" or "I have other commitments." They didn't ask what the time frame would be. The disciples offered their time because His presence was worth it. They dropped everything to follow Him and, in doing so, made themselves vulnerable in so many ways.

They left their jobs, homes, and families and embraced a life on the road. Never knowing when they would see their loved ones again or when their next meal was or if they would have a bed to sleep in that night. They trusted their friend, though. They knew He was worth giving everything for. They knew He would not let them down.

He knew the importance of their bonds. He knew His friends would need memories of their time together to walk the narrow path, knowledge that only He could give, and community after He was gone. He had a purpose for their interactions. The parables He told and the places He took them. When they met someone or healed someone, or even when they took time to go away for rest. Jesus intentionally curated experiences to craft lifelong bonds with Him, with their Father in heaven, and with one another.

They broke bread and drank wine together. They listened to Jesus's teachings. They walked together and talked together. The disciples wrestled with their doubts and asked hard questions. They healed. They prayed. Together, they rose in the morning and rested their heads at night near one another. They lived in constant community.

Jesus's relationships with His disciples changed over time. There is no way they were the same from the moment they met Him until they saw Him rise from the grave. They endured betrayal. Heartache. Denial. Exhaustion from hours and days spent ministering. They didn't know where they were going from one day to the next. They didn't understand the plans of the Lord, even if He tried to teach them in parable. They had to be flexible because they knew the relationship was worth it.

They may not have understood what was going to happen, or even the significance of all they participated in at the time, but they knew in their hearts and in their spirits that there was nothing better this world could ever offer them. They understood that waking and sleeping and eating and talking and praying and walking alongside Jesus was the best gift they would receive in their day. And that being able to do this together was worth it, too. Even with their differences. Because the closeness they were developing with Him and with one another would revitalize their souls as they drew nearer to His kingdom come— here, on Earth. Their relationships spurred them on to share the gospel message of His love and ministry, both when they walked alongside Him and after He had gone to be with the Father. This time spent in the company of the Lord and each other deepened their faith as they wrestled with their doubts, insecurities, and questions and saw prayer after prayer answered in the most miraculous and awe-inspiring of ways.

Making Friends Like Jesus

When I moved to Tennessee, I knew that for new friendships to blossom and grow into what my heart desired, I had to be willing to do the same as Jesus and His disciples. I had to invest my time, be intentional with my actions, have the courage to be vulnerable, and be flexible.

Invest Time

Jesus asked His disciples to drop everything and follow Him, but what was He asking of me when we moved? I knew I needed to invest my time, but I couldn't drop everything like the disciples—after all, I wasn't going to follow my neighbor like they followed Jesus. My time investment had to work with our lives.

After prayer and reflection, I realized I didn't have to invest all my time. I didn't have to dedicate hours each day to reaching out to the neighbor or the woman I met at the grocery store. Instead, an hour every week, or every other week, or even once a month could have amazing results when it came to creating bonds. So we started searching for a church. I joined a MOPS group. I tried forming connections on the bleachers and with neighbors passing by on the trails near our house. I became the room mom at the elementary school and started volunteering at the middle school. I invited friends to dinner and to my back porch for a glass of wine. I carved time in my schedule to find people I could relate to.

What about you? What are ways you can invest your time to develop relationships where you reside today? Is there someone at work who you have felt you could develop a friendship with? Could you ask her to eat lunch with you one day this week? I know that may sound scary or a bit uncomfortable. It may feel a bit like when you were little and you had to go to school on the first day, unsure of who would be in your classroom, not certain of what the year ahead would be like, wanting to make friends and not being sure how. Being friends as a grown-up really isn't all that different. Remember that inner child. Find the time. Make the space. Extend the invitation. Join the club. And if the club you're looking for doesn't exist where you live, start the club. You can do it. You just need to carve out the time and show up. And if the thought of doing this makes your stomach feel all topsy-turvy, know that's perfectly normal, too.

Courage, Dear One

Closeness isn't going to happen with just a quick wave as you drive by in your car. Closeness requires intimacy, and intimacy requires courage—a willingness to put yourself out there and an openness to the possibility of getting hurt.

When I was looking for friends, I did the most unlikely of things. There was a neighbor who moved into the cul-de-sac across from our home who I had seen outside multiple times. As I drove past her one morning, I thought, *I would like to be her friend.* So I walked up to her door, rang the bell, and introduced myself.

I had no idea what would happen. She could have said that "it's not a good time" and promptly slammed the door in my face. She could have looked annoyed that I was showing up unannounced, interrupting her time. Instead, she opened the door and apologized: "I'm so sorry. I haven't brushed my teeth yet. I think my breath smells." She covered her mouth, her eyes smiling above her hand.

I knew we would be close friends. I wanted to hang out with this person who was so honest with a complete stranger who rang her bell. I asked for her number. To this day, her name is listed the same way it was when I entered it on her doorstep: Tara Neighbor Shea. But the thing is, she isn't just my neighbor anymore. She is now one of my closest friends. But that may not have happened had I not had the courage to step out of my comfort zone. That may not have happened if I had let all my nerves and insecurities get in the way.

It took courage for me to walk up to her door, but it was worth it. And I have to believe it will be worth it for you to step out of your comfort zone, too. You may feel socially awkward. You may believe the lie that nobody is going to like you as you are, with your quirks, your messes, your past, or whatever mental barrier stops you from developing friendships. You may be scared to let someone in and to show them the real you. You may fear rejection and heartache. And I get it. I've been there. I know it's not easy. But the best relationships in your life will form when the walls and the façade come down. The deepest and truest and most impactful personal relationships happen when you are courageous. When you show up with your bad breath and your dirty clothes and your unwashed hair—or your polished nails and designer shirt (because this may be truer to you)—and say, "This is me. Here I am."

Showing your full self takes courage. And courage is where the most tender, honest, and compassionate of relationships are formed.

Step out, Dear One. Find the courage and believe what you are looking for will be waiting on the other side of that door.

Be Intentional

True friendship happens when we invest our time, brave unknown landscapes, and are intentional in the ways we gather. If we want to grow close to someone, we need to make space for deep and meaningful connection and conversations.

One of my favorites ways to connect is through walks, coffee dates, and long, drawn-out dinners that last for hours. There is something about lingering at a table that I find to be incredibly intimate and fulfilling. In these spaces, I can really listen and learn about the person I am spending time with. I can get to know what makes them tick and come to better understand what's happening in their life and their heart.

Once I started meeting new people in Tennessee, I would text, email, or call my friends to join me at the local coffee shop in our small town or the new trail I found. I would invite them to join my husband and me, or our entire family, at our home.

To sit at our wooden table gifted to us by my mother-in-law and share a home-cooked meal. Instead of just "catching up," I would dig into their lives. Ask questions, listen intently, and share from my heart. Through these conversations, we learned about past heartaches, childhood stories, and our faiths and beliefs. We better understood where we each had come from, what mattered to us, what made us tick, and the things we hoped for our futures. With each interaction, we learned to trust each other a bit more. We went to the honest and raw spaces of our hearts and, in doing so, birthed true friendship.

If the idea of one-on-one makes you feel a little squeamish, you could always consider joining a Bible study or starting a neighborhood Bunco club—an easy-to-learn dice game that is more about gathering with friends than anything else. Even in large groups, it's still very possible to find your people. Having a heart-to-heart at Bunco may be difficult, but there is something to be said for the friend you can laugh with for hours, too.

Invest your time, be brave, and be intentional. As you do so, you may find connection you never dreamed possible. You may find the relationships you had always dreamed of having, but never knew how.

Flexibility Is Key

As I developed meaningful friendships, I had to remember to be flexible. Just like seasons, relationships shift and change. If I was open to the change, then I could watch my hard-earned bonds mature and blossom into something beautiful. Something full of grace and understanding. Something that says, "I see where you are, and I respect your boundaries and the way you are trying to juggle the demands in your day, even if that looks different than it looked yesterday." Something that acknowledges we are all trying our best in the spaces where we operate and that those spaces change. And that's okay.

I have learned over the years that this piece of the friendship puzzle is of the utmost importance. Without it, some of the seemingly best relationships can crumble. Our lives are not meant to be stagnant, and the same is true for friendship. When someone has a baby, they probably won't be as available to talk as they once were. When someone is married, they may not be free to meet at the gym every day after work. When someone starts a new job, they may not be able to gather for the weekly lunch date. It doesn't mean they don't care anymore. It doesn't mean you're not worth it to them. It just means life has changed.

When my children were very young and I was living in Indiana, I would gather regularly with friends for playdates. The playdates were every bit as much for me (if not more) as they were for my children. During this time, I became the master of the start-and-stop conversations. Do you know the ones I'm talking about? You start talking and then you have to change a diaper or grab a snack, so you leave for five minutes, and then come back and continue right where you left off. My friends and I were highly skilled at those talks.

In that season, our getting together looked like friendship, love, and service. We were very intentional. We would schedule playdates, offer to watch each other's children for an hour here and there to give each other breaks. We would even drop off meals, coffees, and other items on doorsteps for those unpredictable days—like when all your children are suddenly sick and you find yourself unable to leave the house for days or even weeks.

We would text each other regularly to check in and pray with and for each other as needed. I knew I could rely on these friends for anything, at any hour of the day. They were my village. And I can't imagine getting through those early years of child-rearing without them.

As I have grown and my children have grown, my friendships

have grown and changed, too. Now, I am no longer having the start-and-stop conversations, and the need for front-porch coffees and meal drop-offs isn't as great as it once was, but my need for friendship has not diminished. Now, it is lunch dates, evening get-togethers, morning walks, Bible studies, Bunco, serving with friends at schools and our community group. My relationships still require intentionality. They still require putting myself out there, but the avenue for gathering has changed, just as I have changed.

Your relationships should not be stagnant. Allow your bonds to have permission to change, just like with everything else in life. Flexibility is key.

If you hear all this and are longing for more meaningful relationships beyond a quick "How are you?" before the garage door closes, or beyond small talk on the bleachers at the ball game, I encourage you to put yourself out there. I encourage you to set aside some time to connect with someone regularly. Pray over that time. Ask the Lord for wisdom and discernment.

Leave your garage door open a little longer. Make eye contact with the person you see every week at the grocery store. Send the text and don't worry what the person will think of you—maybe they've been praying for a friend, too.

Give the gift of your time. Be intentional. Have the courage to say hello. Be flexible.

Trust He will provide.

Rhythms of Return

Prayer

Heavenly Father,

Help shift my gaze to You and to others in my life. Help me to not be so inward-focused and so quick to close my door. Guide me toward a countercultural lifestyle that returns both to You and to friendship with others. Because I am made in Your image, to be in relationship with You and those You have placed in my life.

God, help me to live fully into those relationships.

Give me space to invest my time in the lives of those around me so I can form deep connections. Help me to have courage to reach out when I am uncertain of the outcome. To step out in faith knowing You have gone before me. Give me wisdom to live with intentionality when it comes to my friendships. To call. To text. To check in. To respond in the ways that share Your love and Your heart and Your kindness. And make my heart flexible to the ever-changing and ever-evolving nature of my life and the lives of those around me.

Holy Spirt, guide me.

Amen.

Questions for Reflection

1. What does true friendship mean to you? Do you feel you have this in your life?

2. When have you seen and felt the power of friendship in action? When you think back to this time, what stands out to you?

3. What does it mean to you to be intentional in your relationships? Can you think of a time when you were intentional? What did you do? What were the results of this intentionality?

4. Is there a time in your life when you had the courage to say hello to someone and that resulted in close friendship? On the flip side, was there a time when you had the courage and then felt rejected? How has this played out in your friendships today?

Invitation to Return

One Minute: Take a minute to acknowledge and thank God for all the deep, meaningful friendships in your life. If you don't feel you have those relationships currently, ask God to help you to form them.

One Hour: Spend time journaling about how you can invest your time and be intentional, courageous, and flexible in your relationships today.

One Day: Schedule a day of friendship. Think back to what you wrote in your journal and go out of your way to connect with friends. Maybe start the day going on a hike through the woods or walking through a museum or other local attraction in your city. Then meet someone for a pedicure or manicure and end the day at a dinner with friends. Be intentional with your time. Put yourself out there. Send the invitation and spend a day connecting.

10

RETURN TO KINDNESS AND GENTLENESS

How to Love the Unlovable

When we love a person, we accept him or her exactly as is: the lovely with the unlovely, the strong with the fearful, the true mixed in with the façade, and of course, the only way we can do it is by accepting ourselves that way.

—Fred Rogers, *You Are Special: Words of Wisdom for All Ages from a Beloved Neighbor*

I have definitely had seasons in my life when I have been more unlovable than in others. My mom actually refers to a period of time when I was a teenager as "the black years." She insists I wore all black, all the time. While this didn't really happen, I think that's how she remembers it because my mood, my attitude, and my sass at that time probably left a dark residual stain everywhere I went. The more I think about it, "the black years" is actually very apropos for that time.

Those weren't my only dark years, though. There have been plenty more. Some of my darker stories hold many things of which I am not proud, but also many things God has redeemed. Each of those moments of darkness has collided with the light. I have seen ashes turned to rubies time and time again.

During my senior year of college, I was in a downward spiral that made my "black years" look pretty rosy in comparison. I was sliding down, down, down into the darkness. And as I slid, I did what people often do in those spaces: I hurt people. I left a path of destruction in my wake.

I chose to hurt the person I was closest to: my best friend, my boyfriend, my future husband, Patrick. Which I guess makes sense in some weird and twisted way. We tend to hurt the people we love the most when we are living in places where our number one concern is our own selfish needs and carnal desires.

Patrick and I had been together since I was seventeen, and although I knew deep down that he was who I wanted to spend my life with, I had a darkened view of marriage. I was convinced that if I didn't see what else was out there, I would be fated to a life of second-guessing and wondering what I may have missed. I thought the only way we could have a future together decades down the road was if I broke up with him. So that's what I did.

I broke up with Patrick, but my heart was conflicted, so our breakup was filled with confusion and contradictory messages. I told him I didn't want to be with him, but I called him daily and asked him to still hang out with me. I wasn't willing to remain in a monogamous relationship, but I didn't want to be away, either. I lied to him. I cheated on him. I hid things from him. I played with his heart and his mind so I could continue to have whatever I wanted.

Yep. I was that nightmare of a person we tell our friends, children, and anyone else who is in the dating world to run from. Run away now. Run as far as possible.

It hurts me to this day to think of how I hurt Patrick, and I'm also amazed. I'm amazed at the grace he showed me and the grace he continues to give. Most people would leave and never glance back, and for a little bit, he did, but the Spirit inside nudged him to return.

The Spirit who moved him back into my arms is Someone I return to when I am faced with the unlovable people of the world. Because through Him, all things are possible—even change. I know firsthand. I'm a walking example.

I had broken Patrick's trust, so, naturally, there were consequences that followed my actions. He had a hard time trusting me again, which meant I had to show him with both my words and my actions that I had changed. Even when those who loved him and were concerned for him told him—as was completely justified—that he was making a horrible mistake to ever trust me again. But Patrick believed in me. He was patient with me, and after some time apart, he gave me another chance.

I moved to Indianapolis to be near him and show him I was committed to the relationship. We went on dates and spent time talking about the hard things. And, most importantly, we really committed our lives to Christ.

Patrick and I had grown up in the same small Indiana town and had gone to the same small Catholic church, but we hadn't been committed to attending church for quite some time. While we were mending our relationship, we both rededicated our lives to God and found a church to call home and a small group to attend. We slowly but surely immersed ourselves in our faith.

Patrick saw a change in me. He learned to trust again. And with his heart full of trust and our love renewed in ways neither of us knew were possible, he got down on one knee and proposed.

We were ready to take this next step in our relationship, down the aisle and into our forever. We believed we were healed from the hurt and the pain and the deception. But when we were going through premarital counseling, our pastor, Jeff Krajewski, informed us otherwise. He realized there were some wounds from our past that needed to be dealt with before we both said "I do."

Patrick had unanswered questions. Questions he was hesitant to ask and questions I really didn't care to answer. But Pastor Jeff knew we needed to walk through this valley for our marriage to start with a clean slate. He told us we would know we had fully moved forward in forgiveness when we could talk about these things from our past with no negative emotions attached.

We weren't there yet, but we agreed that was where we wanted to be.

Pastor Jeff suggested that we set aside a specific time for me and Patrick to meet and ask God to heal our past hurts. We would cover our meeting in prayer ahead of time and ask our friends to pray as well. But we wouldn't engage with anyone but each other and the Lord during that time.

During this set-apart time, Patrick could ask me any questions he wanted to about that dark period in my life, and I would answer honestly, no matter how hard that might be. We then would pray for the Lord to take whatever was brought forth from the darkness to the light, and trust that He would take it. We would believe that those things from our past would not impact our relationship any longer.

Pastor Jeff told us, "If you're willing to trust God and do this, then He will heal any hidden hurts."

I was skeptical. How was Patrick going to look me in the eye and ask me his questions? And how was I going to look him in the eye and answer directly, knowing all the pain I had already caused? How could we bring all that stuff up and then expect it to not have any impact? Surely talking about my sin would have negative consequences. I loved the thought of stripping away the emotions from our past, but reliving it seemed like we would be attaching even more emotions. I didn't want to go there. But my heart knew Pastor Jeff was right. Because I longed for Patrick to fully know me and love me anyway.

The older I grow, the more clearly I see the depth of longing people have to be both known and loved. We want to know we are lovable and that nothing will exclude us from that love. We want to know we can show up as we are, with all our imperfections, and still have a seat pulled up to the table—a seat reserved just for us. We want to know we don't have to work to hide our flaws. That we can mess up and sometimes say the wrong thing, and even do the wrong thing, and that we won't be thrown out the door just because of the mistakes we made. We want to be both fully known and fully loved.

These desires are embedded deep within our souls by the One who knows us more intimately than we know ourselves and loves us more than we can begin to fathom. God created us with these wants and needs, and He is the truest fulfillment of these wants and needs. When we return to Him—when we open our hands and hearts and receive this deep soul desire to be known and loved—then we are better able to give and experience so much goodness in our lives.

The more I have come to see how much the Lord loves me, with no strings attached, regardless of my past mistakes or future mishaps, the easier it becomes to answer the call to "love thy neighbor." And my neighbor isn't just the person who lives next door to me, or around the block in my neighborhood. My neighbor is anyone I encounter. It's the man who works as the crossing guard at the elementary school, who waves me into the parking lot every day. It's the woman who takes my order at the coffee shop. It's the friend who invites me to go on a walk. It's my sisters and my brother. It's the one I call my best friend.

And it's the one I don't care to spend much time with.

But what about *that* person? What about the one who is hard to love? What about the one who is judgmental? Or the one who makes you feel less-than because your house or car or clothes will never be as nice as theirs? What about the one who rarely looks your way when you try to say hi? Or, even more so, the one who has deliberately been unkind to you or, even worse, unkind to your children? What about the one who has broken your heart and your trust?

What about them?

Yes, friend, they are your neighbor, too. And you are called to love them.

Return to Jesus

Patrick and I did what our pastor instructed us to do. We sat in my small apartment and walked through the dark, hard, hidden spaces of the heart that I wanted to forget and he would probably not like to hear. Patrick asked the questions he had been holding in the recesses of his mind, and I answered, worried that he wouldn't forgive me. Worried that he wouldn't love me. But God works in mysterious ways, and as those answers came to light, Patrick instantly forgave me.

My heart swelled. Patrick had known me—my successes and now my deepest failures—and he had chosen to forgive and love me anyway. What I thought was impossible, God had made possible. He moved mountains to heal our relationship. Supernaturally. Forever.

To this day, Patrick lives with grace and mercy. He deals with things as they arise and does not bring them up to use against me later. He forgives me and moves forward with me in love and grace. Patrick models Christ's love, and that is the love I want to give my neighbor.

I want to love in this sacrificial way that is filled with grace and a kindness that penetrates the heart. I want to love in a way that reflects the truth that God can supernaturally heal and that there is incredible power in prayer. I want to be loved and love in a manner that reflects 1 Corinthians 13:

Love is patient, love is kind. It does not envy, it does not boast, it is not proud. It does not dishonor others, it is not self-seeking, it is not easily angered, it keeps no record of wrongs. Love does not delight in evil but rejoices with the truth. It always protects, always trusts, always hopes, always perseveres.

Love never fails.[1]

You are given an invitation each day to meet with a God who loves you in this way. To turn your eyes to Jesus and wrap yourself in an infinite love that is patient, kind, protecting, trusting, hopeful, and persevering. To be filled to the brim with Love.

As you accept His unending love, you may find it becoming easier and easier to love those who are not quite as lovable. Those who have wronged you or hurt you. Those who are not kind to you. Those who do not think like you or act like you or believe in the same ways you do.

You may overflow with His supernatural love so that it seeps into those you meet day in and day out. The teacher at school. The coworker who steals your lunch. The annoying person on social media who always posts their political opinions (which are different than yours). The person on the corner of the road with a cardboard sign asking for money, or the one screaming at you on the street corner. The person delivering the groceries or Amazon packages to your door. The neighbor you wave to every day as you drive by.

You may find yourself seeing others and treating others differently than you ever have before. You may find that you don't need to prove your point as much. Or argue your truth as loudly. You may discover compassion and empathy for those your heart was otherwise cold to.

This radical kind of love is not the way the world teaches us to love. It isn't a tit-for-tat kind of love. It isn't self-serving. It does not come from us. And we know this. We can sense it. We can feel it. Because when our response turns from one of anger or judgment or condemnation or belittling to "How can I pray for you?" or "What is it you are going through to make you act this way?" or "How can I serve you right now?" then we know this reaction is from the Lord.

God can change our hearts of stone, soften our reactions, and fill us with His supernatural love. This transformative love has the potential to change our homes, our neighborhoods, our communities, because His love can move us from prayer to empathy to service.

Love and Boundaries

Years ago, when Patrick forgave me in an instant for all I had done, we both knew it was from the Lord. There was no other explanation. As he prayed for me, God softened his heart. Patrick began to see the pain I was living in and, even with all the hurt I caused, he saw past my mistakes and remembered who I had been to him for all those years. I broke his heart, and yet his heart still broke for me. Isn't that incredible? He wanted to see me get better. He wanted to see us together. And, after all that pain, every time Patrick called me, or took me on a date, or held my hand, he was offering my heart a service.

When you find yourself unsure how to extend love to someone who is not easy to love, start with prayer. Ask the Lord to give you a heart of empathy for this person. Ask the Lord to really show you this person, to break your heart open for them.

People make bad choices for a lot of reasons. They are tired. They are hungry. They are thirsty. They don't have enough money. They have been beat down physically or mentally. They feel trapped. They are looking for an escape. They are oppressed. They have tried something that has slowly consumed them and are now living in a place of addiction. They are lonely. They are desperate. They are without a home. They are without a family. The potential reasons are too long to list here.

Yet understanding the *why* of someone's bad choices doesn't negate the natural consequences. It doesn't mean we excuse unhealthy behavior. It doesn't mean we allow them to behave in whatever manner they see fit. But it may give us some compassion. It may open our hearts to pray for them and to not be so quick to judge them. Taking a moment to see the world from their perspective may give us empathy that we wouldn't otherwise have.

And then, maybe, just maybe—if the Spirit inside gives you a nudge—that empathy may propel you to serve. To have compassion for someone who has wronged you, and then to take that one step further into service, is contradictory to what the world will tell you. But serving our enemy is a powerful witness to the world and to our own hearts. To invite them over for a cup of coffee so you can learn more about their story. To discover a need they may have and then meet that need is countercultural. But maybe, just maybe, that act of service will break that person's heart wide open.

But what happens when our desire to share Christ's love with others puts us in danger? What happens when relationships turn toxic? Friend, sometimes there is forgiveness and reconciliation, and sometimes there are moments when we have to say goodbye.

Patrick's love for me when I was at my most unlovable has been one of the most impactful, Christ-modeling, heart-mending, transformative experiences of my life. He believed I could change, and by the grace of God, I did. But had I not, Patrick would have been foolish to stay. Had I kept cheating on him, lying to him, and all the other things I was doing to his battered and bruised heart, then staying with me would have caused even greater damage to him.

As we talked about previously, some relationships cannot move forward in the space they reside. We can love someone and want what is best for them but also know that our love does not justify being in an unhealthy relationship with them. We can love someone and take care of ourselves by not allowing toxic patterns to cause us harm. We can pray for someone and hope that they change, and if that time does ever come, then we can choose to pursue a healthier relationship with them once again.

In her book *Good Boundaries and Goodbyes,* author Lysa Terkeurst says:

> We all need grace when we mess up. But we also need the awareness that there is a difference between an occasional slip in behavior and an ongoing pattern of behavior. Let's be completely honest with ourselves and those who can help us discern what's the best way to respond and move toward healing. If healing is possible together, then take that path toward peace. But if healing isn't possible if you stay in relationship with this person, then take a separate path toward peace.[2]

Goodbyes aren't easy, and knowing the right time to walk away from a relationship is hard. For anyone who has ever had a relationship with a loved one end, you know there is a deep grieving that occurs. You mourn what is lost and what you hoped would be, but you also know, with the way things are, that there is no way to move forward. As Terkeurst says, the way toward peace is separate paths.

The addict who doesn't want to get clean.

The spouse who won't stop having the affair.

The compulsive liar who refuses to tell the truth.

The one who abuses with fists and words.

The manipulator who twists reality and leaves you upside down after every conversation.

You can love them. You can pray for them. You can want what is best for them. Your heart can be broken into a million tiny pieces as you cry an endless stream of tears. And you can choose to walk away. The walking away isn't a sign that you have stopped praying or loving. Sometimes, leaving is the answer to prayer and the best way to show love. You're maintaining healthy boundaries and recognizing the toxicity of the relationship while also lifting that person up to the trustworthy, gentle arms of Jesus.

If you find yourself in a relationship that is unhealthy, I encourage you to seek counsel. Talk to a mental health professional, a close friend, a mentor, a pastor, or a family member you trust. And if you are in a situation with abuse, do not wait one more second. Get out. There are resources available for you and people who want to help you.

Setting boundaries with those you love is not easy. Letting someone know the behaviors you will no longer tolerate is a hard conversation. And making the choice to walk away after the boundaries have been set and violated can break your heart in ways your heart has not been broken before.

But sometimes, that is what is necessary.

If you are in that spot today, I pray for you. I lift you up. I ask the Lord to fill you with wisdom and discernment and that you will be surrounded by wise, godly counsel who will help you take whatever next steps are needed.

Yes, we are called to love our neighbor.

And sometimes, that love looks like boundaries.

Sometimes, that love looks like walking away.

I pray that in your moments of conflict and pain with the one who seems most unlovable, you will clearly see your next steps forward. That Jesus will guide your steps and fill you with wisdom and discernment as you move forward in empathy and service, or as you choose to walk away.

Return to Jesus. Lay the hard relationship down at His scarred feet. Trust He will light the way for you and show you the next steps. Friend, lay it down and believe that He will, because He can move mountains.

Rhythms of Return

Prayer

To the One who knows me and loves me anyway,
Thank You for loving me when I have slid down,
down, down into the darkness of my life. Thank You for
modeling to me what this love looks like.

Help me to see others as You see them. Spirit, nudge
me toward prayer for the unlovable. Show me when
my heart is hard. Break my heart open and fill it with
empathy for the ones I do not long to be with. Show me
ways to serve the hard-hearted.

Give me wisdom and discernment and strength to set
necessary boundaries and to walk away if needed.

Bless my relationships.

Fill me, Lord. Let that love pour out and all around.
Just as You have loved me.

Amen.

Questions for Reflection

1. What does it mean for you, personally, to love your neighbor?
2. Is there a time in your life when someone showed you great love and grace, even though you don't feel you were deserving of it in that moment? How has that impacted you?

3. Has someone ever performed an act of service for you that you weren't expecting? How did this make you feel?

4. Have you ever helped someone, or served them in some way, and then found your heart change for them? What about this experience stands out to you most?

Invitation to Return

One Minute: Is there someone in your life you are finding it difficult to be in a relationship with? Say a prayer for that person today. Ask the Lord if there is a way you can serve them. Ask Him if it's time to walk away. Trust that He will make a way for you and that you will know the next steps.

One Hour: What would it look like for you to reach out to the unlovable person you're dealing with? See what's happening in their life? Ask questions, listen, and affirm their struggles? If you can safely engage with that person, then reach out to them to find out. If you aren't in a space where you can engage with them, then take some time to imagine different things your neighbor could be going through. How might it feel to be in their shoes? Use this time to write down your thoughts.

One Day: Make a list of tangible ways you can perform an act of service for your neighbor. Consider mowing a lawn, baking some cookies, watching young children so the parents can have a date, or inviting someone to your home to share a meal or play a game. Pick one idea and a day to do that in the week ahead.

PART THREE

COLLECTIVE RETURN

More people have been brought into the church by the kindness of real Christian love than by all the theological arguments in the world.

—William Barclay, *New Testament Words*

11

RETURN TO UNITY

Will They Know We Are Christians by Our Love?

Be united with other Christians. A wall with loose bricks is not good. The bricks must be cemented together.

—Corrie ten Boom

A t the end of February 2020, our friends, the Sproulls, were visiting from out of town. We gathered around the kitchen island and talked quietly, yet sincerely, about what was transpiring on the news. Another four cases of the coronavirus had been detected in the States. The most recent cases were in California, on the other side of the country from us.

I mentioned my husband had just made a trip to Costco as a precautionary measure. Our friends wondered if they, too, should consider stopping by Costco on their drive home to stock up on toilet paper and other essentials. Surely this was all over the top. This would probably be overkill, just like all that water I bought before the Y2K prediction of a global downfall. I mean, what's the likelihood we would ever actually run out of toilet paper? But just to be safe.

In the week that followed, we were doing the things we usually did, but there was a tension in the air. Word of the virus spreading across our country traveled from news sources into our homes and workspaces. Conversations were heavy and filled with anxiety. We didn't know what was coming, but something was.

At that time, I was a preschool art teacher, and on March 5, one of the teachers came into the classroom and whispered to me that the coronavirus had made its way to our county. Within minutes, a text notification alerted us that school would be canceled the next day—as an extreme precautionary measure. You could hear all the phones pinging simultaneously with the news. *Ping. Ping. Ping.*

The talk for the remainder of the school day was mostly about the pandemic. People were apprehensive yet still excited to have the day off. *Would there be more? What did this mean?*

That day turned to two. Then, the next week was cancelled. And then the week after spring break. Suddenly, my husband was working from home. We all were home. And that day we all were excited to have off stretched out before us into one endless day. We wondered, When would we return? And if we did, what would that even look like?

The global anxiety was growing. We had no way of anticipating what was to come. Not only in our homes, but also as a society. We were used to contention. Things had been heating up politically for a few years, but this only added fuel to the political fire. The talk now was of social distancing, masks, politics, vaccinations, and other polarizing topics. The tension was thick. Lines were drawn in the sand. Which side would you stand with? Were you in? Or were you out? Were you for us? Or were you against us?

Family members turned against family members.

Neighbors against neighbors.

Friends against friends.

Christians against Christians.

All the dissension. All the screaming. All the nasty comments typed in haste and fueled by emotion filled my social feeds. It was getting so very loud out there.

When did our politics become our faith? With one word—democrat or republican, masked or unmasked, vaccinated or unvaccinated—we deemed the person worthy or unworthy. Faithful or unfaithful. Trustworthy or untrustworthy. Wise or foolish. Friend or foe.

I wrestled with this myself. When the pandemic began, I found myself glued to the news. I had to know what was happening. And the more I watched, the more my anger grew. I was trying to find unbiased news sources but kept being drawn to those who thought the same as I did. And the more I watched those who thought just like me, the more convinced I became that I was right.

My social feeds and news channel were feeding me more and more and more of my own beliefs. There was no neutral. It was all polarizing. And the more I scrolled and saw the nasty comments and the people who loved Jesus like me but thought differently, the more frustrated and confused I became. How could we see the world so differently, yet hold the same faith so close to our hearts?

I wasn't feeling unity with many of my fellow believers. On the contrary, I wanted to distance myself. They were demonizing me. And I was doing the same—maybe not externally, but internally.

When I first became a believer, I was drawn to the notion that other believers were called to love me as I was. Because the Lord loved me as I was. As a recovering perfectionist bent toward people-pleasing, this idea of love for the sake of love was incredibly appealing.

But I wasn't seeing this love anymore. Instead, I saw lines drawn in the sand. More and more people yelled, "You need to think like me." More and more people declared their way of seeing Jesus and worshipping Him and interpreting Scripture as the only way. And anyone doing anything else, or thinking any other way, had fallen prey to the enemy.

What happened to our love? Where was our unity in Christ? Were we reflecting our love for one another despite our conflicts, differences, and viewpoints? Were we showing the world that we are humble, gentle, and patient with each other? That we can bear with one another in love? Or were Christians screaming the loudest?

Return to Jesus

Sometime in 2020, I realized I had to pull back. I had to stop watching the news. I had to stop the scroll on my phone. I had to ignore comments in the comment section.

I just couldn't anymore.

I needed Jesus.

I made returning to Him a rhythm and practice. I disconnected from the political and social chaos swirling around and dove into the Word, connecting with God. I journaled more and spent time in prayer, silence, study, and contemplation. I prayed for Him to silence the noise.

I sifted through the rubbish, clung to the truth of my faith, and held tightly to the anchor of His love while the winds blew all around. I asked hard questions: "What do I do when someone who loves the Lord, too, sees the world so differently than me?" "What do I do with this animosity that is being spewed in the name of Jesus?" "How do I respond when someone is aggressive with me because I believe differently than they do?"

As I practiced the return to His gospel message and spent time in His presence, I read about Jesus gathering with His disciples on the eve of His death to issue a new command:

Love one another. In the same way I loved you, you love one another. This is how everyone will recognize that you are my disciples—when they see the love you have for each other.[1]

God convicted my heart. He loved me *and* the person at church who spoke out against my heart. He loved me *and* the person who left inciting comments on my posts. He loved me *and* my neighbor who voted differently than I did. He loved each of us—with all our flaws and all our shortcomings and all the ways we messed up—and He commanded me to love others the same.

I didn't need to judge. I didn't need to understand the intricacies of the human psyche or ethos. I didn't need to convince someone else why I thought I'm right or why I thought they're wrong. I needed to love, even the difficult ones, as Jesus loved me.

That is how they will know we are Christians—by our love. Our love is how we are different from the world. How we stand apart. Or at least it's how we are supposed to be.

We can get trapped in our algorithms and forget that Jesus's love and grace is for everyone. We can yell and scream; post unkind, furious words; and miss the person on the other side of the screen. We can condemn everyone who believes the opposite of what we do and forget the love we're meant to share with them. We can walk away from a relationship because our worldly beliefs aren't lining up and we don't want to associate with people who see the world differently than we do.

When we seek out Jesus, though, we remember: we all have fallen short of God's glory, and we all have been washed clean by His blood.[2] We all are loved equally by our Father above. All of us who call Jesus our Savior and believe in Him are called righteous.[3] When we look up to Jesus, we can show one another this love we have been called to share.

I know. I know. Spreading His love and gifts is much easier said than done, especially in our politically fueled society. And none of us will get it right all the time, because none of us is perfect. But where do we even start? How do we show love to someone who sees the world differently than we do? Where do we find common ground?

Friend, we find commonality in Jesus.

As Paul told the Ephesians:

Be completely humble and gentle; be patient, bearing with one another in love. Make every effort to keep the unity of the Spirit through the bond of peace. There is one body and one Spirit, just as you were called to one hope when you were called; one Lord, one faith, one baptism; one God and Father of all, who is over all and through all and in all.[4]

We have been called to keep the unity of the Spirit. To be united with one another from this place of universal love. We can stand side by side and hand in hand with our different beliefs because of the one same belief we hold in Jesus. There is one body and one Spirit. We are the body of Christ.[5] We are the temple of the living God.[6] Jesus's Spirit resides in us and through us. His Spirit makes it possible for us to be humble, gentle, and patient as we bear with one another's differences—because we hold the same Spirit within. While we may not vote the same, or see the world the same, or think the same, we are all called to hope in Jesus. We all love Jesus the same. And He is within us. When we ask for less of us and more of Him, this is where we will find unity.

As we look to Jesus, we can weigh our personal beliefs against

His truth. We can honestly examine our hearts and hold them up to the light of Scripture. We can ask ourselves hard questions like "Am I making idols out of my beliefs?" and "Are any of my beliefs harming others in the name of Jesus?" Nothing is above reproach. Nothing is above examination. And we can pay close attention to those answers, because our faith should not be a weapon against a person or a group. Our faith should never be a catalyst for hate, exclusion, or bigotry. Our faith should always reflect love for all persons.

Jesus is love, and when we accept the invitation to return to Jesus's love, redemption, healing, grace, and restoration, then we open our hearts and minds to be changed. We remember that our brothers and sisters are not the enemy. We look up for the answers, then look out at the world with His heart to embrace true unity.

A Heart After His

I have scrolled through social media and felt my blood boil. I have seen posts that made my stomach churn. I have felt anger burn inside me at a comment about Jesus that is so diametrically opposed to the Jesus I worship and love. I have thought, *I don't want to be lumped in that category. When I say I follow Jesus, I don't want people to think I follow Jesus like that.* I have wanted to attach a disclaimer to my faith.

But then I pause. I breathe deep. I return to the Jesus I know and love. I return to Scripture. I pray. I ask for His peace to cover me. I remember it isn't my job to change anyone else's mind.

I am released.

Released to move forward. Released to stop the ruminating thoughts. Released from the need to prove my point. Released to love.

When confusion from the noise of the world threatens to take hold, return to Jesus. Step away from news and devices and other things that may harm relationships instead of helping them. Avoid social accounts that get your blood boiling. Instead, replace the scrolling and angry conversations with time spent in Jesus's presence. Breathe in His peace, exhale His love.

Hold on to the truth that every person you encounter is an image bearer of the Almighty. Even if you don't think the same. Even if you don't agree. Even if you don't particularly like them. God does. And that makes them worthy of love.

Christlike love looks like sitting across the table from someone you love who thinks the opposite of you, and not needing to change them. It's showing them respect. It's listening to them. It's not shutting them out because of differences, but rather inviting them to share a meal.

His love looks like silencing your pride and realizing that you don't have all the answers. We all have a lot to learn in this world, and to think we know it all would be foolish. If you shut out everyone who thinks differently than you and stop listening to opposing sides, you may be missing out on teachable moments in life. You may be missing out on the opportunity to learn new things and to embrace new truths—as long as those truths are not hateful or harmful.

When you intentionally turn away from the division, anger, and screaming and return to love, then you will find unity, too. You will find it by praying for instead of arguing with your brothers and sisters who feel differently about the world than you do. And not praying for God to change them or to make them see everything the same way you do. But just for them. Where they are. As they are. In their humanity, with their joys and with their struggles. You will find unity when you actively find ways to love other people and go to them instead of condemning them and pushing them aside.

So when your thoughts get tangled and your mind becomes

pseudo-obsessed with a post or a comment you just *know* is wrong, ask God to take the need for fingers-flying-over-keyboard combat away from you. Ask Him to silence the loud and angry thoughts. Ask Him to help you hold space for those who aren't the same and to give you wisdom to do so.

Ask Him to help remove any anger. To keep your mind and heart from judgment. To fill you with wisdom so that you know when to use your voice and when to remain silent.

When you don't know how to face your friend or sibling or parent or neighbor because you're in opposition to how they see things in the world, ask His Spirit inside you to intercede and fill you with the supernatural love that comes from Love Himself. Ask God to hold your tongue if it will cause harm. Ask Him for a heart like His.

Pursue unity.

Rhythms of Return

Prayer

Dear Heavenly Father,

There is a noise in the world that rattles the windows and shakes the walls of our foundations. It is loud. It is deafening. It is anger and yelling and dissension. It is me holding on to my personal beliefs and convictions more than the belief and convictions that come from You.

I wear my pride like a badge of honor.

I enter a room puffed up and ready to attack the first who comes against me. Conservative. Liberal. The way I identify. I will fight for these.

But do I fight for You?

The fight for You is not to fight as the world fights. It is to lay my life down for those I love.

Through my prayers, I fight for You. By holding space and honoring those who are not the same, I fight for You. When I am slow to speak, slow to anger, slow to judge, I fight for You. When I have discernment to know when to be silent and when to speak, I fight for You.

Let me fight with unity.

Not with dissension.

Every person who wakes and breathes and sleeps and dreams is an image bearer of love. May that love flow through me and out of me as I am humbled in heart and silenced of pride.

May I love as I am called to love.

Not just those who think like me, but all.
Amen.

Questions for Reflection

1. Think of a time when you have felt unity with others. What is something you notice about that time? What do you think it means to be unified with others?

2. Jesus loves all His children with the same love. What would it look like for you to extend a Christlike love to others?

3. Have you felt like it's loud out there? What are some ways you cope with the noise?

4. Have you experienced a time when you felt dissension with another believer because of a difference in political or cultural beliefs? What does Jesus say about that person? This may be a hard question, but be honest: Is it hard for you to believe Jesus feels that way about them, too? If so, why might this be hard? Could it be possible you have made your political or cultural belief your idol?

Invitation to Return

One Minute: Is there someone you have lashed out against over the past years because of your differences? Pray for guidance on your next steps in this relationship. Ask God how you may be able to move forward in love and unity with this person.

One Hour: This activity may be harder than others to face, but is there someone, or a group of people, who you have made your enemy? Have you forgotten that they, too, are loved by God? Take an hour today to be in silence with this. Go on a walk. Sit outside. Lie on the ground. Ask the Lord to transform your heart for this person or group. Think of who God is and what it means to be made in His image. Ask Him to show you this person as He sees this person. Take the time to go to those hard places in stillness and in quiet, knowing the Lord will meet you there.

One Day: Do a news check. Do you find yourself scrolling, or watching, the news a lot? Is this biased news, or unbiased? Ask God to show you if you need to take a break or limit your time because it's affecting your love for others. If He's calling you to a break, be faithful to take that break and notice any change that takes place in your heart during your fast from the news. If you aren't drawn to the news but are regularly on social media, then do a social media check instead. Are you following people who incite division among believers? Accounts that make them forget Jesus's call to unity and love? Spend the day going through who you follow and asking God which accounts you need to unfollow.

12

RETURN TO A LIFE FREE FROM JUDGMENT

I'm a "Good Christian" Girl and You Better Be, Too!

*You Pharisees and teachers are in for trouble! You're nothing
but show-offs. You're like tombs that have been whitewashed.
On the outside they are beautiful, but inside they are full of
bones and filth. That's what you are like. Outside you look
good, but inside you are evil and only pretend to be good.*

—Matthew 23:27–28 (CEV)

Sometimes, I drink one too many glasses of wine.

Sometimes, I eat one too many gluten-free Oreos.

Sometimes, I watch shows that I know aren't the best for my
mind and spirit.

Sometimes, I get angry and swear.

Sometimes, I put my windows down and sing loudly to lyrics
that most definitely aren't appropriate and hope nobody is
around to hear me when I roll up to the stoplight.

Sometimes, I skip church for no other reason than the fact
that I want to sleep in.

Sometimes . . .

Sometimes, I do things that aren't the best for me. I do things that erect a wall between me and God. I do things that create distance between me and my loved ones. I do things that block me from my community. Actions I wish I hadn't done. I wake up in the morning and think, *Ugh. What did I do that for?*

I'm not proud of these "sometimes" choices. I don't hope for these things in my life. But I'm human. And sometimes, I'm stressed, exhausted, or just having a cruddy week, and these poor choices happen more than I care to admit.

Early in my Christian walk, my mission was to eliminate all these unsavory behaviors from my life. I had to be pure. I had to be clean. I had to be righteous. I had to always behave, in all situations, around all people. After all, I was now a living, walking, breathing testimony. And sure, I had made mistakes before when I was in the deep, dark pit of my past, but now, well, now there just wasn't room for any of these mess-ups.

I had to stay on the straight and narrow path because that was how I would show others I was true to my faith. I had to follow the rules because that was how I would be judged. So I wouldn't drink. I would only listen to Christian music. I would only surround myself with others who believed the same as I did. I would use caution when watching TV shows and movies.

I was on fire for Jesus, completely engaged in the Christian lifestyle, constantly looking for ways to share His love and bring people to His kingdom like a "good Christian" girl should. The list of service at that time in my life was long. I was doing the things I felt like I should be doing to prove my strong commitment to my faith. Quiet time: check. Host a Bible study: check. Serve others: check. Attend church: check.

Don't get me wrong, these things were good—these things *are* good. It's good to pay attention to what we consume with our bodies and minds. It's good to eliminate behaviors that create a barrier between us and God. It's good to strive to be obedient to His calling on our lives, but these actions always go back to the heart, and my heart was starting to tarnish. My heart was shifting from sitting with Jesus and letting His love and grace flow in and through me to a heart that was focused on what my faith looked like from the outside. What was I doing to prove I belonged here? What was I doing to prove I deserved a seat at this table? Was I checking off the right boxes?

And, slowly, without an awareness that it was even happening, this straight and narrow path I had to walk became my measuring stick for my faith and the faith of others. Were the people around me checking off the right boxes? Were they proving their holiness to the world with their actions?

I would scan a room, and if I spotted someone making a choice that seemed a bit off, I would think, *Oh, I should ask my group to pray for them* or *That's too bad, they must be slipping away.*

I couldn't see the harm I caused with my judgment. I justified sharing details of someone else's life through prayer requests, but they were just pious forms of gossip. I elevated my "righteousness" above other people, internally shaming their choices and saying a "holy" prayer for them, but never seeking them out. Never asking how they were doing or how I could help. I scanned for behavior I had eliminated from my own life, locking on and silently condemning while forgetting all the grace bestowed on me when I did the same things.

Legalism had settled in my spirit. A black-and-white faith with no room for error or mistake had crept into my heart. If you love Jesus, you (fill in the blank). If you do (fill in the blank), then you must not love Him as much as you say you do.

I wasn't being taught these things at church. Not at all. But I was young. I was zealous. I was maybe even a bit prideful. And, at that time, I didn't have a lot of older, wiser people speaking into my life.

I was entering a dangerous territory. One where I was forgetting that we all are convicted of our own things at our own times. One where I wasn't acknowledging that we all fall short—even the one who appears the most pious. One where I wasn't considering that we all are traveling our own roads, with our unique temptations and struggles we fall prey to.

Many Christians before me have lived in this territory, many reside there now, and many more might unintentionally join later. In this place of legalism, only people committed to following the rules can walk through the door. Only righteous actions matter, not the love we are called to share with our neighbor. We pick and choose which sins to ignore and which ones deserve wrath. We elevate ourselves in an outward show of commitment to the law rather than sit and abide with the One who came to fulfill the law. And as a result, our eyes and words become daggers we throw.

Instead of trying to invite others to rest in the shelter of our Savior's wing, we are creating lists of all the things that need to be done "right" before someone walks through our congregation doors. We are searching for reasons others should be "out." But this legalistic faith does more harm to the Body of Christ than good, even with all that goodness we are attempting to project into the world.

Have you found yourself there? Have you ever been in a state of holy exhaustion, becoming increasingly frustrated with those around you because of their inability to step up and help when there are so many needs to be met? Have you thought, *They must not be as committed to their faith as I am*? Have you ever looked at someone and said, "I haven't seen you in church or at group for a while," but your internal thought is, *I wonder if they're slipping away?* Have you seen someone with a drink in hand, heard about a show they're watching, or seen the company they're keeping, and thought, *They must not be as strong in their faith as I am,* without knowing anything else besides what you see with your eyes?

If you've answered yes, you are not alone. So have I. I am not asking these questions to point fingers or cause guilt. I am asking because I, too, have been there. I know the ease with which these questions slip into our minds. That is, until I was the one regularly missing church. Until I was the one no longer attending the prayer meetings. Until I was the one no longer able to make our small group regularly. Until I was the one who could no longer serve in all the ministries I once served in.

I checked off the boxes until life did what life does, and I found myself in a place where the boxes could not so easily be checked off anymore. With sleepless nights, nursing infants, and what seemed like never-ending rounds of sickness between the now six members of my family, I couldn't perform as I once did. The self-righteous me of my twenties was being challenged by the spit-up-stained me of my thirties.

My ability to perform was stripped away, and I found myself in a posture of surrender. With grace and kindness, God helped untangle the mess I had unintentionally found myself in. He asked me to take a good, hard look at myself, urged me to re-examine the heart of my faith, and taught me to give grace to my "sometimes" and the "sometimes" of others. And He reminded me that I am not called to judge. I am called to love.

A love that doesn't hinge on how good we are or how good other people are. Doesn't hinge on how put-together everyone in our church seems on a given Sunday. Or on how well we eliminate the "sometimes" in our lives and the lives of those around us. My job isn't to "fix" you and set you on the straight and narrow path. And your job isn't to do the same for me.

I don't know about you, but I can happily say, "Thank goodness for that."

Return to Jesus

God does not require a list of boxes to be checked off in a state of holy busyness. He simply requires me to sit at Jesus's feet, listen to His Words, walk the path He walked, and answer His unique call in my life. Jesus isn't asking me to work harder *for* Him or to find people to change in His name. His yoke is easy. He wants me to simply be *with* Him.

In this way, my faith is my personal relationship with the One who has numbered my days and my hairs and my freckles and the stars that blanket the sky. I have a story that is unique to me. Temptations unique to me. A family unique to me. And convictions unique to me. Because of my individual experiences and personhood, I understand and know Jesus differently.

The same is true for all of us. Every person we encounter at the PTO meeting or at work or sitting next to us on the airplane has a unique set of circumstances that will be reflected in their faith walk.

Since we are all unique, God comes to us differently. We see this truth reflected in the life of Jesus. He healed a blind man by simply stating, "Your faith has healed you."[1] Then, in another interaction, He spat in the dirt, spread the mud across another blind man's eyes, and told him to go bathe to be healed.[2] In some instances, Jesus healed and then instructed the person to tell no one.[3] At other times, He said to go and tell their family and friends.[4] Jesus met some people in their homes and others in the streets. Some He found in their greatest time of need, like the woman who was about to be stoned, and others when they weren't even aware that they needed Him at all. Jesus was constantly approaching people based on their individual needs.

I may be convicted tomorrow to start listening to only Christian music again, but that doesn't mean that the same conviction now applies to every single person I see on a given day. God placed that conviction on *my* heart, not on everyone's heart. And a year from now, He may say, "Okay, listen to secular music again." Because in the flow of love, things change, things move. How Jesus guides us may be for a season to help us grow and deepen our relationship with Him. The season may be forever (especially if you struggle with some form of substance abuse or addiction), or the season may be just for a little while. Only God can tell us what season we are in and where He is convicting our hearts.

The Sadducees and the Pharisees could not see beyond their instruction into the heart of their faith. They were unmovable and pious. They had learned the way to follow Him with their doing, but not the way of sitting in His loving presence. They saw one law. One set of rules. One way of living. They had been taught their entire lives to live with their eyes open to the coming of the Messiah, but when He arrived, He was different than they imagined. He didn't do things the way they expected.

Jesus challenged their laws and their rules. He threatened their way of life. Their status. Their wealth. Their power. Their security. He allowed His disciples to not wash their hands before they ate.[5] He healed on the Sabbath.[6] He broke bread with sinners.[7] He drove out bad spirits.[8] He hung out with the unsavory and performed acts that were unclean in religious leaders' eyes.

When Jesus talked to the Pharisees, He said:

> You make God's law to mean nothing so you can keep your own laws!
>
> You are not true to yourselves! What Isaiah said about you was true. He said,
>
> "These people respect me with their mouth but their heart is far from me.
>
> They do not mean it in their hearts when they worship me. Their teachings are only the words of men."[9]

These religious leaders were so focused on appearing to be good, on following the laws, that their hearts were far from God. They weren't connected to the Holy One and so they couldn't see the Savior when He was right in front of them.

Can you imagine? Jesus walking down Las Vegas's strip talking to the money launderers, sharing a meal with the strippers, and calling to the kids drawing graffiti on the sides of buildings, "Come to me." Never condemning, always loving, always inviting them to join Him.

When we live, we look to Jesus as our example, not the religious leaders. We sit at His feet and learn from him. We walk with Him. We treat people like He treated people, with compassion, love, mercy, gentleness, kindness—longing for their healing. Instead of daggers and self-righteous thoughts that wonder what they must have done to make them fall so far and hard, we offer grace and loving hands to pick up our neighbor who has fallen. We remember all Jesus has done for us and long to share with others a taste of the sweet grace that has nourished our soul. We remember our need for Jesus and look to His life for how to live. And when we do, Jesus will be with us.

God With Us

In my twenties, I was regularly *doing* for the Lord. In my thirties, my babies and the demands of my life shifted, and I could no longer *do*. I had to learn to sit. To *be*. I had to learn that missing church didn't make me bad. That calling off the house church we hosted because our babies were sick didn't make me bad. That the exhaustion I felt deep in my bones from sleepless nights that kept me from opening the Word as much as I wanted didn't make me bad.

I had to learn my devotion to my faith and my Jesus wasn't about my strength. It wasn't about how "good" I appeared to those looking in from the outside. It wasn't about proving my faith to anyone. It wasn't about my performance. My faith was about my walk with the Good Shepherd, the One who leads and guides His flock.

If I relied on my own strength, answers, and ability to get everything right, then my Shepherd wasn't leading me. If I wandered off to do it all on my own, then I wasn't following His command. If I was more concerned about the rules and the law than being in a loving, committed, connected, abiding relationship with Jesus, then I was listening to my own voice, not His.

I began to understand that nobody has a right to judge me and my walk. This was between me and my God. And in this place of surrender, my relationship blossomed and grew. My faith wasn't about what I was doing for Jesus. It was about sitting with Him. I sat with Him while changing diapers. I sat with Him while nursing my babies and cleaning up vomit in the night. I sat with Him through the long days when my husband was out of town and I wasn't sure how to do it all on my own. Because in the end, I needed Immanuel—God with me.

As I communed with Jesus in my quiet place, I began to understand that just like nobody has the right to judge me, I do not have the right to judge them.

When you aim to live like Jesus did, then you'll walk like He walked. You'll notice someone hasn't been at church for a while, or you haven't seen them at Bible study, and you'll call them to find out how they are doing. You won't try to convince them to return, nor will you spread their business in the form of a "prayer request." Instead, you'll listen and let them know you love them, wherever they are and in whatever they are going through. You'll live as Jesus did, and the world will see Jesus among us.

When we give Jesus our legalism, then we move out of a place of judgment and condemnation and into a place of seeing the world with eyes of mercy. We stop trying to be everybody else's

Holy Spirit, and we live our lives authentically, humbly, and sincerely, with the Lord at the center. We spread love, give grace to others, and live in peace because we are rooted in something so much bigger than the things of this world.

When we spend time with Jesus, asking Him how we can be His light in this dark world, He fills us with His Spirit. We embody joy, kindness, faithfulness, and all the fruits of the Spirit. He moves through us and pours from us as we walk the halls of our homes, our workplaces, our neighborhoods, and our schools. And the world will say, "What is that? I want that!"

When we release the judgment in our hearts, we go beyond the prying eyes looking out at an unjust, corrupt world. Instead, we seek to empathize, to listen, and to understand. We walk as Jesus walked. We become reflections of His goodness on Earth. We become vessels of His love.

As you interact with those in your community—the person who just ordered their fifth margarita, the neighbor who has decided church isn't for them anymore, and the person who you think may be hiding an affair—remember to check your thoughts. Remember they each have a story you aren't privy to and a faith walk just for them. Do not try to fix them, save them, or point out the choices you don't agree with in their lives. Instead, see them as Jesus does: a precious person whom He loves.

Friend, live as Jesus lived. Dine with the outcast, embrace the sick, and let your heart break for the lost. Come alongside others in their struggles, and remember when others did the same for you. Because you will not always get it right. You'll still have your "sometimes" moments, but remember, life with Jesus isn't about being "good."

So pursue Him and get to know Him. Invite Him into all the places and spaces of your life and rest in His presence. Sit with Him in the wee morning hours, the lazy afternoons, and the busy evenings. Release the need to work for Him. Recognize the convictions on your life, hear His voice, and lay down those things He is calling you to lay down—and recognize those are yours, not everyone else's.

Walk as Jesus walked. Talk as He talked. Breathe, eat, and speak a life of love. And in all things, pursue life with your Shepherd at the lead.

Rhythms of Return

Prayer

Jesus,

I want to do good. I want to be good. I want You to see me and to say, "Well done, my good and faithful servant." But sometimes I get swallowed up by all that goodness I am striving for, and my good becomes my downfall. Sometimes, the good I am in pursuit of is no longer simply You, but my own checklists, boxes, rules, and ideas of how being a Christian is supposed to look.

Sometimes, I work and strive and move forward, but I still throw daggers at people I am sure have fallen prey to their wrongdoings. Sometimes, I am no longer full of grace. I am full of judgment.

Take this condemning spirit from me, Father. You are the author and perfector of my faith.

I do not want this ugliness I find myself spewing in Your precious name.

May I always see others as You see them. May I scan the room looking for someone to extend hands of love toward—as You have always done with me.

May I not make the goal be how good I am, but simply how well I loved.

In Your mighty name,
Amen.

Questions for Reflection

1. Do you feel you are in a place where you are struggling with legalism? What would it look like to give that legalistic spirit to God?
2. Do you feel you have been judged by others for not being "good" enough? Do you feel you are hard on yourself for not being "good" enough?
3. This may be a hard question, but can you relate to the Pharisees or the Sadducees? Has there been a time when you were more focused on the way others were following Jesus than on how you were following Him yourself?
4. This is another hard one, but do you feel you have measured another person's faith by the "goodness" in their life? What did this do to your relationship with that person?

Invitation to Return

One Minute: Pray for the Lord to show you any judgment or legalism you are harboring in your heart. Give this to Him. Ask Him to take it from you today.

One Hour: Have you ostracized or treated someone poorly because you felt they weren't checking off the right boxes or were not "good" enough? Ask God to remove the legalism you placed on their faith and show you how you can reconcile with that person. Do you feel led to apologize? Can you invite them for dinner? Or maybe write them a letter? How can you make amends and acknowledge the pain you may have caused this person today?

One Day: Spend the day rooting out your assumptions about being a "good Christian." What does it mean to you to be a "good Christian?" Jot down things that come to mind. Is this something you feel you are striving for? Ask the Lord to help you lay this at His feet, and trust that He will. And if there is something you are doing that is past the point of expiration because you feel it makes you "good" in His eyes, take the courageous step to eliminate that thing for this season. Now that you have sorted through your assumptions about being a "good Christian" with the Lord, mark a day off to simply sit with Jesus. A day to get into the Word, study, and learn what it means to live a life like Jesus. Create a list of ways that Jesus lived to learn more about how He is truly calling you to live.

13

RETURN TO FREEDOM

The Heavy Burden of Silence

Even the darkness is not dark to you;
the night is bright as the day,
for darkness is as light with you.

—Psalm 139:12 (ESV)

When I was nineteen, a freshman in college with dreams and ideas of how my life was supposed to stretch out before me, I sat in the small downstairs bathroom of Patrick's college home. Perched atop the cold, white porcelain toilet with a generic store-bought pregnancy test in hand.

I sat staring at the stick. Two dark lines showed up in an instant.

Wasn't it supposed to take longer?

There was no question. I was pregnant.

For the weeks that followed, I agonized over what I should do. *Do we keep the baby or don't we?* Back and forth and back and forth and back and forth . . .

Was I considering the unforgivable sin? I had heard about the way people yelled and screamed as women walked in and out of clinics. I saw the billboards on the highway. I had received the message loud and clear: If you make this choice, you deserve to be condemned. If you make this choice, you are a horrible human. Unworthy of love. Unworthy of grace.

I lay in bed sobbing. I wasn't sure how I would go through with it, but it felt like the only thing I could do at that time in my life.

I made my choice. I had an abortion.

For so long, I struggled to forgive myself. For so long, I struggled to believe I could be forgiven. I knew abortion was what some hung their hats on in the voting booths and made their missions to fight. By fighting my choice, it felt like they were fighting me. The message I received, whether intended or not, was that my choice had cast me into the lot of the unlovable—a lie I deeply believed about myself.

I wanted so desperately to lay down my choice and accept the forgiveness Jesus offered, but I just couldn't. I was completely stuck. There was no budging. But I was weighed down by more than just the guilt, more than just the unlovable label I placed on myself. I was wrapped in my shame and didn't know how to unwrap myself from it.

The shame defined me, so I guarded my secret at all costs. But, looking back, it held me captive. It became a silent stone around my neck that I carried with me wherever I went. It kept me from sharing all of my heart and all of my story. It kept me from the deepest, truest relationships I could have. It kept me from fully connecting with my community.

Years after my abortion, while still residing in this space of shame and silence, I attended a weekend retreat called the Indianapolis Great Banquet—a place for people to disconnect from their daily demands so that they can learn more about Jesus and His great love for them. The retreat took place inside a magnificent, massive old brick church with chapels full of colorful stained glass. Over the weekend, a large, framed picture of the face of Jesus traveled with us from room to room, which in a way made it seem even more like He was there with us. His soft eyes always watching.

With my notebook and pen in hand, I sat listening to the closing remarks of a talk. I looked at the picture and wondered what Jesus thought of me. He knew my choices. He knew my secret. He knew, but nobody else around me did. I had made sure of that.

The attention shifted from the speaker on stage to the individual tables as we began our group discussion. I looked at the women gathered around my table and thought over and over again, *I can share my truth. I can talk about the dark places I've gone. The substance abuse and the eating disorder and the lying and cheating and promiscuity—but I must omit this part.*

I was committed to the burden of silence.

Later that day, I sat in the hallway across from a girl I was just getting to know. I felt a connection to her and was hoping we would build a friendship. I wanted so badly to open my mouth and let the words tumble out: "I had an abortion." I remember thinking, *Just tell her.* But the words were stuck in my throat.

I would later learn that, had I told her, I would have discovered I wasn't alone with my secret. She shared the same story. I would have learned how common this story is among Christians. But we never talk about it, so how would we know?

So I sat in silence, feeling alone even in her company. I sat in silence, longing to say the words without any clue that this person would have offered me comfort and, instead of condemnation, would have said, "Me, too, friend. Me, too."

As the weekend went on, I would meet and talk with people, but I couldn't fully connect. Women shared their truths, cried into Kleenex, offered hugs, and found relief from sharing long-held secrets. But I couldn't do the same. I found myself growing frustrated or jealous at how easy it was for all the other women to share. If I shared my full story, they would judge. They would see me differently. They would shun me and walk away. No, I couldn't tell them.

Keeping secrets is exhausting. Keeping secrets takes work. Keeping secrets harms relationships and stops us from building strong connections. Keeping secrets makes it harder for us to walk in the freedom God gives. Keeping secrets builds walls and puts us in bondage.

Maybe you have a secret, too. Maybe it's a choice you once made, or still make. Pornography. Adultery. Substance abuse. Addiction. Chronic gambling. Binging and purging. Compulsive and chronic lying. Maybe it's something that was done to you. Molestation. Rape. Physical or mental abuse—maybe both. Something so horrible you've endured that you have never been able to share.

What would it take for someone to have access to that space inside you? Does the thought alone fill you with unease, maybe even dread? Does the weight of your secret pull you to silence?

Up until a few years ago, sharing about my abortion was too hard. I would have shared every other story in my life without a second thought, but not this. It felt too raw. Too vulnerable. It had too much potential for judgment and icy glares or comments fueled by anger from others. I believed my choice would define me more than anything else.

And that's how it is with those unspeakable secrets that take hold of us in the dark and threaten to slowly consume us. They trick us into believing if people knew, then our lives would fall apart. If people knew, we would not be loved. If people knew, everything would change.

But the thing that we often forget, or at least I do, is that what matters most is the opinion of God—and, my friend, God has always known. He knew the choices you would make before you even breathed your first breath. He knew that thing you have locked away would happen. Jesus knew He would carry that thing with Him to the cross. When everything fell on His shoulders, that thing you don't dare speak about fell on Him, too. And He took that dark blemish with Him and washed it white as snow.[1] And never once, for one second, did your secret change how He felt about you. Nor will it. You are worth it to Him. You are worth giving His life for.

For always and forever.

We work so hard to hide the unspeakable parts of our stories. But when we turn to Jesus and His abounding love for us, then we find freedom. We can look at someone and think, *It doesn't matter what you think of me. You can judge me. You can dislike me. You can throw your stones, but that doesn't define me.*

You are not what other people think. They cannot define you. Your stones do not define you. Only God can define who we are. And He says you are forgiven. You are loved. You are not alone, because He has never left you. He was with you in that moment you work so hard to hide. He is with you now.

Friend, there is freedom at the foot of the cross. Freedom to release your secret. Freedom from condemnation. Freedom to go deeper and develop stronger bonds with those you love. And yes, freedom in sharing. Freedom in finally speaking those things we are afraid to speak. But to experience this freedom, we need to hold that thing we are bound to up against the truth of Jesus, not the condemnation of the world.

Return to Jesus

I had done so many things of which I wasn't proud. So many things I once swore I would never do. Things little me, playing outside in the sandbox and splashing in the cool water of Walloon Lake, could never imagine in her life. Substance abuse. Promiscuity. Hurting those I loved the most. Abortion. Then, once I started sliding down those paths, my judgment became cloudy. One thing led to another that led to another, and I woke up one morning filled with a heavy shame, wondering how I got there.

In a space of grappling with my shame and my fear that I had fallen too far for the grace of God, I began to go over verses and stories that spoke of Jesus and His love for the marginalized,[2] the oppressed,[3] the outcast,[4] the widow,[5] the orphan,[6] the woman,[7] and the sinner.[8] He loved in a new, profound, and radical way that caused the religious leaders of the time to be blind to who He was: God in the flesh in their midst.

As I learned more about this Jesus and His love for the unsavory people of His time, I started to think, maybe, if Jesus were here, I would be one of those unsavory He would choose. Maybe He would be at the clinic, too. Only, He wouldn't be screaming at me. He would be holding me. He would be tender with me.

He would be weeping with me.

This revelation blew up my world.

The more I leaned into Jesus and His truth, the more I came to see that He did not want me to have a spirit of fear, but of power, love, and self-discipline.[9] Not fear that binds, but power that comes from walking in His truth and love. Not fear of sliding down a path where I have lost all control, but freedom that comes from self-discipline.

God was asking me to let go of the fear that my secret would be discovered. But He didn't expect me to do it alone. He sent His Spirit to comfort me and hold me in those fearful moments. He gave me a way forward. A comforter to hug my soul and my heart as they healed. A helper to reside in me and guide me. The third part of the Trinity. God within us.

The same is true for you.

Jesus will hold you. He will love you. He will walk with you through the depths of the valley and up to the other side. The Comforter will intercede for you and your soul in ways that go beyond what you ever knew you needed. He will make a way when it seems there is none. And when your secret bursts forth into the light, He will be right there with you.

You may be thinking, *This all sounds great, but it's just not possible. The shadow my secret casts is just too dark.*

Friend, I am sorry for the thing you went through. I am sorry for the pain you hold. Know, though, that there is nothing too dark for the Light. Jesus came to bind your broken heart, lift the heavy weight of your secret, and release you from the darkness.[10]

The beauty is that so often, when those secrets are revealed, the opposite of what we thought would happen happens. What *really* consumed you was the thing you were working so hard to hide. Once you're released from your secret, your shackle is removed. You breathe easier. You move lighter. You walk in freedom instead of in fear of what may happen if your secret is discovered. Your relationships can be renewed as you uncover what it means to be in community without secrets.

A few years after that weekend retreat, I took a big leap forward in my healing. I joined a Bible study specifically for women who had had an abortion. I met weekly with other women who had made the same choice and kept the same secret. It was there, in the small library of the church basement, where I discovered that the community I had been avoiding was exactly what I needed for my healing.

We would sit on hard folding chairs in a tight circle, unraveling our deepest secrets. We would share our stories, our pain, those stones we wore around our necks and the shackles around our limbs, then measure up our shame against the Truth of God. We would invite His Spirit—the Comforter—to join us. Week after week, walls came down.

I was healing. I was starting to understand that this choice did not keep me from the love of Christ, and even though some may judge me, He would not. He did not leave me in that moment, and He wouldn't leave me as I spoke my secret outside of this trusted circle.

As I told a few close friends, weeping each time I recounted my secret, I started to see what this study was teaching me week after week: Healing takes place when things are brought forth from the darkness to the light. Healing takes place in communities that are focused on the love of Jesus.

At the study, they encouraged us to share our stories with more people. They encouraged us to ask the Spirit inside to move and show us when and where was the right time to crack open our vaults and begin living in this freedom we all longed for.

They encouraged and I prayed, but it felt impossible.

I had held on to my secret for so long. Outside of this small group of women and the few people Patrick and I had told, I couldn't seem to get the words out. I met with a friend for coffee, but the words wouldn't come. I congregated weekly with our house church—a group of friends from church—but my secret remained on the tip of my tongue. I wanted so badly to share, but then I would remember how everything might change, and I would stuff the words back inside where I was certain they belonged.

Until one day at church when, in the most unlikely of ways, the Holy Spirit moved, and I found myself in a place of surrender I never expected.

Community Without Barriers

It was a typical Sunday morning at our small church in Indianapolis. Our house church had been assigned childcare duty for the 9 A.M. service, so we attended the 11 A.M. service together. Nearly our entire group was there, and we slowly filed into the sanctuary, taking our seats next to one another.

The worship began as usual, and our voices lifted in unison to the familiar songs we had grown to love. Standing next to me was Jenn, my best friend to this day. As Jenn began to sing, tears poured from her eyes and rolled down her cheeks. I turned to look at her and asked what was wrong.

"I don't know," she replied.

She looked genuinely sad and confused as the tears fell one after the other. My arm wrapped around her shoulder, and we continued to sing.

After the music stopped, we took our seats and our pastor stood to speak. He said to the congregation, "Today, I am doing something different than I've ever done before."

My heart started beating. Hard. Why was I so nervous? Usually a statement like that wouldn't illicit this kind of response.

"Today, I am going to pass the microphone around and let anyone who feels led to speak, speak." He went on to talk about the Holy Spirit inside each of us, and that if we started to get a fluttery feeling, maybe we should pay attention to that nudge and consider sharing whatever was on our heart.

Oh no, I thought. *This is a flutter. Isn't it? Oh no.*

This cannot be happening.

The microphone was passed as person after person raised their hand or stood to let our pastor know they felt led to share. And the fluttering inside me grew stronger and stronger. My palms grew sweatier and sweatier. My heart started beating faster and harder.

Oh no. This cannot be how I share.

I steadied my shaking body, wiped my palms on the fabric of my pants, and stood up. My pastor walked over to me with kind eyes. He handed me the microphone.

I took it from his hands.

Okay, Lord, this is happening.

I lifted the microphone close to my mouth. I made eye contact with my friends. God had made a way for each of them to be there for this moment.

"When I was nineteen years old, I had an abortion."

Deep breaths. Don't worry about what people will think. Return to Jesus and His love.

So far so good. I went on to share some more. And when I finally sat back down, my friends hugged me and placed their hands on my shoulders. When the service ended, they surrounded me and my husband. They spoke words of kindness and encouragement.

There was no condemnation. Only love.

My friend Jenn approached me with tears in her eyes and said, "God gave me your tears."

And I knew it to be true. She didn't know why she was crying when the service started. She didn't know what was about to happen, but the Spirit inside her did. I had never told that story up until that point without crying. But in that moment, when I stood in front of the entire congregation and spoke my truth, my voice was strong and my eyes were dry.

I had been praying for a long time about when and how to share, and God provided the most beautiful and unlikely of ways. He went before me and made a way for our closest friends to be there. He gave my tears to my friend and gave me the strength to share in a manner I never could have imagined. And the sweet release, forgiveness, and healing that followed was more than I ever could have fathomed.

I now share my story freely, and nearly every time I share it, someone comes up to me and whispers, "Me, too." Some share freely. Some have revealed to me in a quiet voice that they have not told another soul. And whatever side of the spectrum they fall on, their next words are almost always the same: "Thank you for sharing." And my response is almost always the same: "That was brave. Thank you for sharing."

The enemy wants you to think you are alone, but you are not alone. No matter what roads you have traveled, you have never been alone. And you never will be. Whatever your story may be, whatever your secret contains, there are others who can join you. There are people who can whisper into your ear, "Me, too."

When you find the courage to share your secret, not only do you walk in freedom, but others may start to walk in freedom, too. When we share our story, others may find themselves being nudged to share theirs as well. And when this happens, there is a soul-connection that takes place.

Have you ever sat across from someone you love who shared a hard truth about themselves with you? Have you sat with someone who poured out those hidden things into the space between you? What did you feel in that moment? My guess is you felt gratitude that they trusted you. My guess is that you wanted them to know how loved they are. My guess is that you held them and said thank you—maybe you even found yourself saying, "Me, too." My guess is you felt your connection with them grow even stronger in that moment of sharing than it did in the seconds before.

Sharing our full story creates deep and meaningful connection. And hiding a part of ourselves from those we love can unintentionally create barriers. The same is true with our relationship with the Lord. If we can't confess to Him because we are worried about condemnation, then we won't feel as connected to Him. It isn't that He is pulling away from us, but rather that we are turned away from Him. His arms are open and His gifts extended, but if we are hiding, we won't feel the comfort of those arms or the relief provided by His gifts. But if we go to Jesus openly and freely, with all those parts of our hearts, then the deep well of connection to Him will overflow and the barriers we are consumed by will be brought down by the tidal wave of love, grace, and acceptance.

While sharing your journey is good, not everyone needs to know those secrets you have kept. Ask the Lord to show you who to share with and when. Sometimes, He calls us to share with more people than we ever imagined—like me, right now. But most of the time, it's a handful of close, trusted people in our lives.

As you return to Jesus, there are things inside that you may not even realize you need. Words you don't know need to be prayed. Secrets you may not know need to be revealed. But the Spirit inside you does, and He intercedes for you in ways you aren't even aware. The Spirit helps you in your weakness:

> We do not know what we ought to pray for, but the Spirit himself intercedes for us through wordless groans. And he who searches our hearts knows the mind of the Spirit, because the Spirit intercedes for God's people in accordance with the will of God.[11]

Remember this, and in these moments when you are tangled in your shame and bound by something in your past, return to Jesus simply by saying, "Spirit, help me. Guide me. Take this from me." Confess whatever it is you are holding inside, because the Lord knows. He knows what you need, and He longs to provide for you. He longs to see you freed from those things you are holding so tight—from those secrets you may have locked away inside.

Even if you don't know how to confess, or how to pray, or how to share, or how to even begin to think of releasing this secret, the Spirit inside you knows how to pray, and God above will make a way for your healing. The invitation awaits.

Even if the world tries to condemn you, even if people try to shame you, even if there are people picketing you and your choice, Jesus will not. He will be with you every step of the way.

He will comfort and help you. He will guide you on when and how to reveal the darkness in your heart. And when He does, the stone will fall from your neck. The key to your secret vault will unlock. You'll experience deep heart connections, and your relationship with the Lord will grow.

Step out of shame, friend, and into the glory of freedom.

Rhythms of Return

Prayer

Bondage Breaker,

*Thank You for never leaving me or forsaking me.
Thank You for being with me in my hardest moments.
There is no road I have traveled where You have not
been. I just forgot to search for You. Now, I see You in
those moments. Holding me. Loving me. Caressing me.
Tender God of mercy and love. Son of Man who took it
all to the cross. All of it.*

*Crack my vault open. Loosen my shackles. Remove my
stones. Take away the weight of my secrets. Help me to
confess them to You and lay them down at the foot of the
cross, for always and forever.*

*Show me who I can trust, who I can speak my truth to,
and make a way for this to happen, Father.*

*Let me live in deep connection and community with
others, without any barriers keeping me from being fully
known as I long to be known. And if others judge me,
Lord, help me to know that that is on them. That is not
mine to carry. That is not mine to own. Do not let their
hardened hearts become weights on mine.*

Thank You for dying for me, Lord.

*Thank You for forgiving my sins as far as the east is
from the west.*

I love You, Father.

Amen.

Questions for Reflection

1. Is there something you are currently ashamed of that you haven't confessed to God? Take a moment and confess that to Him now. Do you think there is anything you have done that could keep you from the love of the Lord? If so, please know, friend, there is nothing you could ever do that would keep Him from loving you. I know it takes so much more than me just saying that. Please go to Him in prayer and ask Him to reveal to you tangibly how much He loves you. Make it specific. Trust that He will.

2. Is there something from your past you have never shared with others? What do you think keeps you from sharing this part of your story?

3. Have you experienced deep, meaningful connection with others? What made those relationships so special to you? Do you feel that those people really knew you? And you them?

4. Have you ever been in a relationship and felt like there was a wall that was up? Reflect on that relationship and ask the Lord to show you what that may have been. If it is something on your end, what would it look like for you to help that wall come down?

Invitation to Return

One Minute: Begin each day with a prayer: "Spirit, guide me. I give you this day." Say this before you get out of bed each day, and trust that your prayer will be answered and that He will intercede for you in ways you could never imagine.

One Hour: Ask God to show you anything from your past that you have not been able to let go of. If this is something you have never told anyone, ask God to bring someone to mind you can share this truth with. Pray for Him to prepare their heart and yours. Although it may be hard, trust Jesus with this piece of your past. He was with you then, as He is now. He has never left you or forsaken you, nor will He ever. If the thought of sharing with someone you know is too painful, consider what it would look like for you to talk to a professional about this struggle. Maybe a pastor or a counselor? Can you schedule that hour-long appointment and meet with them? Trust that the Spirit will move you when the time is right and that He will make a way for you.

One Second. One Minute. One Hour. One Day at a Time: Sometimes, the reason we struggle to tell others about our secret is because we are afraid not only of what they may think of us, but also of change. If you struggle with addiction, pornography, substance abuse, financial turmoil, or something else that may require help or support from a professional or organization, like Alcoholics Anonymous, pray for the Lord to give you the strength to make that change. Confessing and stepping into a new life isn't easy, but beauty does lie waiting on the other side. Ask Him to show you if there is someone in your life who can hold you accountable. Even if you aren't ready yet to move forward toward change, commit to praying daily for God to make a way when the time is right.

If this isn't your struggle, do you know someone who does struggle with these things? Someone who has opened their vault and shared the deep and dark places with you? If so, can you reach out to them and let them know you are thinking of them?

Maybe plan a day to connect and see how they are doing. Spend some time in prayer and ask the Lord to show you how to best make that connection.

Lastly, some of us have people we are close to who struggle with addiction that they aren't ready to turn over yet, and this can cause us harm. If this is part of your story, please consider looking into a support group like Al-Anon to begin your own journey toward healing.

14

RETURN FOR HEALING AND GUIDANCE

I've Been Hurt by the Church—Now What?

It isn't necessary that we stay in church in order to remain in God's presence. We can make our hearts personal chapels where we can enter anytime to talk to God privately. These conversations can be so loving and gentle, and anyone can have them.

—Brother Lawrence, *The Practice of the Presence of God*

As a young girl, I watched my mom sit in the pew week after week after week during communion. It didn't seem fair. She didn't even want the divorce, but there she sat, unable to get up when we did.

In Catholic tradition at that time, my parents were required to annul the marriage to participate in this weekly sacrament of wafer on tongue and wine on lips. The sacred time when we remember the Last Supper of Jesus and His sacrifice on the cross. She refused to annul. The marriage had existed. She had loved my father, and she had me and my sister as a result of their union.

So there she would stay as we would rise from the hard,

wooden benches and walk down the aisle to receive our communion. Her mom. Her dad. Her siblings. Her nieces and nephews. Her children. All of us would leave her behind with the pain from her past marked like a jagged scar on her heart.

A bitter taste soured my mouth as I walked down the aisle, away from my mom. I was young, but I was still pretty certain Jesus had died for all of us. All were invited to the table. I mean, He even included the one who would betray Him. If Judas could participate in the Last Supper with our Savior, surely my mom could participate in this weekly remembrance of the supper. Right?

Wrong. She couldn't. And it hurt.

While I had built a good foundation in the Catholic Church, I made the decision early on that it would not be my forever home. I had learned about the Father, Son, and Holy Spirit. I had attended an evening class every Wednesday so that I could learn about the Lord and participate in the sacraments. But these lessons never penetrated my heart. I went through the motions of rising and sitting and kneeling. I sang the songs and recited words and prayers from memory in call and response, but my heart wasn't in it. I lacked a personal connection to the church that had cast my mother aside.

When I left my home for college, I attended mass on the rare occasion when someone invited me to join, or when I messed up so badly that I felt I needed penance. And when I was in my twenties, during one of my darkest times, I tried to attend the Catholic Church again. In my younger years, I had known the inner walls of the sanctuary church intimately and sought comfort from the hymns and the rituals. Sitting in the pews, walking down the aisle to participate in communion, triggered all the feelings I had when I was a child. The hurt crept back in.

I knew this holy place was steeped in centuries of tradition.

Many people made this building their home and deepened their faith. But I also knew this wasn't for me. Maybe one day I would return, but for now, I needed to look elsewhere.

Sadly, I'm not alone in my experience. People around the globe have been hurt by even the most well-meaning, Jesus-following environments. They've encountered pride, envy, greed, hunger for power, lust, self-serving behaviors, and more, because in our humanity, we all fall short. Even the religious laws and traditions that span thousands of years—and, yes, even the one standing behind the podium on Sunday morning—are not immune.

Our pastors and elders lead us, teach us the mysteries of the Bible, and shepherd us in the way we should go. So we place them on pedestals they never asked to be put on because they should know better than us. When our leaders fall, when the façade comes down and stares us in the face, our hearts break. And we are faced with the reality that even the most well-intentioned of people can still make awful choices. Because they are human, too, complete with temptations, flaws, and brokenness.

And the hurt doesn't stop there, because the ways in which the church can trample our hearts is wide and vast. The member of the LGBTQ+ community, the user whose life is being wrecked by addiction, the prostitute, the adulterer, the one who views the world differently than the church does, are turned away at the church's doors. There isn't a place for those lifestyles that don't assimilate well with the values and messages the church adheres to.

And what about the children? We can't possibly have our children influenced by these people. To accept them is to condone their behavior. If the church allows them inside, then we are asking for more of their kind. We don't want their kind here. Right?

Jesus accepted everyone, but we draw our lines of judgment and decide what is acceptable and what is unacceptable, who is in and who is out. It's so backward. And when the imperfect people worshipping our very perfect God get it wrong, it hurts.

So what do we do? Where do we turn to when our hearts are split open by the people we trusted to keep us safe? We return to the only sanctuary who will never leave us, forsake us, or hurt us: Jesus.

Return to Jesus

The religious leaders of Jesus's day held on to their traditions and laws. Like our churches today, they sometimes got it right— bringing life, love, and healing to many people in those days. And other times, those leaders got it horribly wrong.

In Luke, we encounter a woman who had been bleeding for twelve years. When a woman bled, according to the law, she was considered unclean and would have to announce before entering any public space that she was unclean. What would life be like if every time I was on my period, I had to yell "unclean" as I left the house, walked into a grocery store, or hit the gym? Not only that, but if she touched anyone, they, too, were considered unclean. Talk about a horrible game of real-life cooties that never ends.

Can you imagine? When she went to the market to buy food and announced "unclean," did everyone avoid her? When she handed her money to the vendor, did he tilt his head toward a bowl to avoid her touch? What was the Sabbath like? Did she observe the holy day alone? I can't imagine anyone welcomed her into their home or gatherings. I have to imagine all they saw when they saw her was someone who was unclean and unworthy in their eyes. Someone who would rub off on them in a negative way, making them unclean, too.

Ostracized by the church, by its people, by society, and unable to find healing—can you imagine her hurt? We know this woman didn't want to live with this bleeding, because she sought out doctors and healers, desperately seeking healing. Yet her condition remained. Nothing worked.[1] Then she heard of a man who healed the lame and the blind and raised people from the dead. Desperate for hope, longing for healing, she went to Jesus:

> She came up behind him and touched the edge of his cloak, and immediately her bleeding stopped.
> "Who touched me?" Jesus asked.
> When they all denied it, Peter said, "Master, the people are crowding and pressing against you."
> But Jesus said, "Someone touched me; I know that power has gone out from me."
> Then the woman, seeing that she could not go unnoticed, came trembling and fell at his feet. In the presence of all the people, she told why she had touched him and how she had been instantly healed.[2]

How many times had this woman seen people recoil from her touch, from her presence? For more than a decade, she received the same response everywhere she went: distance. And now, here was a holy man—a prophet, some said; the Son of God, others said—someone who was clean, cleaner than anyone else she'd ever met—and she had *touched* Him. She had every right to believe Jesus would respond in horror.

But Jesus didn't respond in disgust. He didn't make her yell "unclean." He didn't reprimand her for taking some of His power without asking His permission. He didn't give all the people standing around a knowing glance of "Can you believe this woman?" No, He responded as He always does, with love, compassion, and healing. "Then he said to her, 'Daughter, your faith has healed you. Go in peace.'"[3]

Jesus accepted the bleeding woman's touch. He acknowledged her presence. The minute she reached out to touch His cloak, He knew. Knew her, knew her need, knew His power could heal her. He didn't recoil from her but reached for her by letting His power heal her. She wasn't abandoned. She was accepted.

The laws of the Catholic Church excluded my mom like the bleeding woman. She had done nothing wrong, but they held her at a distance. Jesus would have drawn her close. He wouldn't have shunned my mom because she was divorced. He would have sat with her. He would have held her. He would have loved her through her pain to the other side. He would have healed her.

I can see now, as a woman in my mid-forties, what I couldn't see when I was a young girl kneeling on the wooden bench next to my family: even though my mom was excluded from communion, she was never abandoned. Jesus was there. He was with us as we took communion and remembered Him, and He was also sitting next to my mom.

Decades later, I now know those rules weren't made to hurt my mom. They were made from a set of beliefs that that denomination held to be true, and I know for a fact that many encounter Jesus every Sunday at that church. Just because it didn't work for me doesn't mean it doesn't work for everyone. I can see now that to hold something against an entire religious group is to ignore the work God is doing there in the lives of countless numbers of His people.

Coming to this place of recognition that that church may be a place where someone else flourishes took time. At first, I struggled. I was mad at my church for many years. All I could see were the tears my mom would cry at night after my dad left, and the image of her head bowed low on Sunday as we all rose from the pew and left her seated.

But as my relationship with the Lord grew, my heart began to soften for the church. As I grasped more and more onto the love of Jesus, His perfection, and our imperfection, I came to see that religion, systems, and laws—anything with humans involved—always have the potential to hurt us. The secret to moving past hurt is to go to Jesus for our healing. To grab onto the cloak of our Lord and let Him carry us through to the other side.

When I went to Him time and time again in Scripture, study, and prayer, He made a way for me to see the gifts of the church under all that hurt. There was a reverence in the ritual. There was acknowledgment of the saints and of the mystery of faith. There was comfort found in our voices lifting the hymns to the heavens, knowing these songs had been sung for centuries. There was the familiarity of the prayers. The reciting. The call and response. The standing and kneeling and sitting. The incense. I realized I found so much peace in those traditions and practices. Jesus helped me sort through the mess to find this beauty. He helped me move from anger to seeing His presence on the empty pew with my mom.

Now, when I look back, I picture Jesus next to her with His arm around her, holding her close with a tenderness unlike any I have experienced in my lifetime. He holds her with His scarred hands and looks at her and says, "I died for you. You are always welcome at My table. My body and My blood are for everyone. None are excluded." Then the jagged scar on her heart evaporates, and all that is left in its place is love.

I have been hurt by the church at times in my life. I have been hurt by members gathering together in His name. I have been hurt by doctrine. I have been hurt by the way I have heard Christians arguing with one another and treating their politics like their god. I have been hurt by Christians talking about, and judging, other people who are God's children, too—even if they make different choices than they do. I have been hurt. Just as I am sure I have hurt others, too.

But the good news is, Jesus heals. When we acknowledge those hurts, speak their name, and take our anger and hurt to the Lord, we can heal. He won't think less of us because of those things we felt. Like all things, He knew all along. But we have to go through it. Not spiritually bypass it. Not pretend it's not there. But walk the path and trust that Jesus will guide us. He will show us when to stay the course and when to start anew.

Guidance on the Next Steps: Return? Relocate? Remove?

When the church gets it wrong—whether because of doctrine that doesn't sit well; a conflict with someone within the church walls; ministry burnout; the exclusion of others because of bigotry, hatred, or bias; or one of the many other reasons a church may hurt—please know you have choices. You can choose to walk away. You can choose to change churches. And, as long as you aren't suffering abuse of some kind, you can choose to stay. All three are okay responses.

Stepping away from a church and saying it doesn't work for you is okay. Disagreeing with doctrine that a denomination holds dear is okay. Switching denominations is okay. Admitting you've been hurt and that a church isn't working for you anymore is okay.

It's okay.

These words and actions don't make you unfaithful. They don't mean you are a traitor. And they surely don't mean you are going to be cast into the fiery pits of hell. Leaving your church also doesn't mean that the church doesn't work for other people. Or that people aren't coming to know Jesus or giving their lives to Him there.

Just like with every other aspect of your faith, deciding whether to stay or go is personal. It's relational. It's intentional. And you need to find what works in whatever season you find yourself in currently.

But how do I know, Jen? How do I possibly decide?

My friend, that's the wrestling. We take the wounds of our hearts to the foot of the cross—to the One whose scars were made for us—and we ask Him: Do we return? Do we remove ourselves altogether? Do we relocate?

I don't know the hurt you've endured in the name of Jesus. I don't know what kind of pain you felt as you gathered with those you trusted and loved. I don't know your story, and I won't pretend that we can unpack all of it in just one chapter. Church hurt is a big bag to open, and we only have so many pages here. But I would love to help get your wheels turning and the prayers started.

The first questions to consider if you are in a painful mess are: Should you return? Is this the place for you? Has this congregation or denomination stopped working for you? Do you walk back through those doors? Or do you find other doors to walk through?

Return

Sometimes, we experience situations where there is no abuse, wrong teaching, or another clear-cut reason to leave. Our hearts have been hurt and we question whether this church is the right fit, but leaving just doesn't seem like the right answer. In those cases, we may find that sticking it out and returning to the place of pain can lead to healing—not only for us, but also for others within the walls of that building.

Perhaps someone within church walls has been judgmental or unkind to you. What if, instead of leaving, you approached the person who you felt was judgmental or unkind and invited them to meet with you? What if you shared your feelings and sought reconciliation? In doing so, you may discover a hidden pain or hurt they were experiencing that caused them to act in a way they otherwise wouldn't have. Maybe they didn't realize they were being judgmental or unkind, and your conversation may lead you both to look at how you are treating others. Maybe this conversation will create empathy and better understanding of one another that will cascade into other relationships.

Perhaps there was a sermon or two that didn't quite sit well with you. What if, instead of searching for a new church home, you ask for a meeting with the pastor to talk more about the sermon that left you feeling uncomfortable? What if you talk about it at a Bible study or a small group? You may discover that your takeaway wasn't the intent of the message, that others felt the same way, or that it was a misunderstanding. You may learn something about the Bible that you didn't know before, or it may help your pastor to consider how messages are being delivered to the congregation. Remember, pastors aren't perfect, either, and your conversation may open their eyes to something they had been blind to before.

Perhaps you felt ignored or like there wasn't a place for you in the ministries the church offered, and you felt alone. What if, instead of leaving to find a church with the ministry you need, you attempt to start that ministry in your church? What if you meet with the elders or church staff to talk about your very real need and the loneliness you have felt in the congregation to see if they may know of others who feel the same? You may discover there are others who have those same longings, and in doing so, you may make wonderful connections at a time in your life when you need them most.

Sometimes, the answer to your church hurt is to return. Like with all things, you'll know when you take your pain to the foot of the cross and trust Jesus to make a way forward. As you wait for His answer, discuss your choices with trusted friends and counsel. Listen to their advice—because sometimes Jesus speaks through people—and weigh it against the Word. Returning to a place that caused pain and healing is possible, and maybe, just maybe, your healing will help facilitate the healing of others in your community, too.

And sometimes, the answer is to leave, especially if abuse is involved. Instead of staying, the Lord may be pulling you to remove and relocate.

Relocate

When I rededicated my life to Christ, I worked with a woman who was on fire for the Lord. Paige was full of joy and would talk openly about Jesus and the good news of the gospel. I wanted what she had. But I was coming out of a challenging time. I had just moved to Indianapolis to help mend my relationship with Patrick and figure out what I wanted to make of this future that stretched out before me. I was on the other side of many poor choices and was making amends with people I had hurt. I was trying to change my life for the better. I knew the Lord but hadn't been living for Him for a very long time. I was confused about things, unsure how to grow my faith, and still holding on to the church hurts from my past.

After sharing my heart with her, Paige agreed to meet with me once a week to study the Bible during lunch. She poured into me and spoke truth into my life. And I shared about my church hurt. I told Paige that I knew I needed community with other believers. I wanted it. I recognized my faith would grow with other believers—iron sharpens iron.[4] Church was where I would find others to pray for me and point me toward the truth of my faith when I needed it most. It was where I would find others who also longed to return to Jesus. But I was scared. Would I be hurt again?

I will never forget what she said: "If you are looking to people for perfection, they will always fall short. They will hurt you, and they will make mistakes. Where you need to be looking is to God. He is perfection. He will not hurt you."

If I was looking for people to give me a reason to walk away from my faith, then I would more than likely find one. I needed to shift my gaze to God, who will never fall short or hurt me. And I needed, in my pain, to remember our collective humanity. There is no such thing as a perfect church on this side of heaven, nor will there ever be.

Her words helped me to have faith in organized religion once again. They opened my heart to the idea of return. They helped me get through the doors. I took a leap of faith.

If you have been hurt and hesitate to return to a faith community, please know you aren't alone in those feelings. I imagine there are many who struggle to go back after being wounded in a place where you go for healing, where you go to grow in faith with a body of believers.

I want to encourage you to keep praying. To keep asking the Lord for guidance. To ask Him to show you your next steps toward community. Because He is calling you to worship and grow with others.

Hear me: God's presence in our lives isn't based on how many times our bottoms meet pews on a Sunday morning or Saturday evening. He isn't counting, and we shouldn't, either. Trust Him to meet you there. You may choose to go back to where you were before. You may choose an entirely different building to worship in. You may choose to meet with other believers in a study group at the library. Whatever you choose, He will be there. Because where two or more are gathered, Jesus is there.

Remove

Sometimes the answer isn't to return to a church or to relocate to another church. Sometimes, the answer is to remove. Sometimes, you need to take a break from these spaces and places after you have been deeply hurt. Sometimes, you need to wander through the wilderness with your God while you figure out your next steps. Sometimes, you need to step away for your heart to heal properly before you can immerse yourself in community again.

I've lived a lot of life in the religious community. And I've heard from many voices that it's wrong to go a single Sunday without attending a service. But we are all unique individuals, with different hurts and different roads to healing. For some, I believe walking away and wandering through the desert—with Jesus by their side—may be exactly what is needed to find healing.

If this is the space you are in, then I pray for your journey. I pray you find support and love in the wilderness. I do not condemn you but pray you hear Jesus's voice as you navigate this dark night of the soul. I pray people meet you on the crossroads to ask, "How are you? How can we come alongside you?"

Because you deserve tenderness, not defensiveness. You deserve love. You deserve hugs. You deserve a safe place to talk about the pain you experienced in church, even if it is uncomfortable. You need to know that even if the building you were choosing to worship in is no longer working, you have not been abandoned. Jesus is inviting you to return.

You were made for community. You were made to worship and gather with other believers, to spur one another on and to encourage each other to return to Jesus and His truth.

Know that whatever choice you make—whether it is to return, to relocate, or to remove yourself for a time while you sort through your pain—Jesus is with you in all of it. He is holding you with His scarred hands.

Just like He was with my mom in her pain.

Just like He was with me in my anger.

Never abandoned.

Always held.

Rhythms of Return

Prayer

Dear Heavenly Father,

I come to You with my heart split open from all the pain I have ever experienced within the walls of the church.

Heal me, Lord. Mend my heart.

Order my steps. Guide me. Show me what path to take toward healing from those hurts I still wrestle with in the night. Make it clear. Do I return? Do I relocate? Or is it my time to wander with You through the wilderness of my faith, trusting and knowing You are always with me and that I can worship You wherever I may reside?

I trust You, Lord.

I believe You will make a way for me to enter into community again.

I thank You, Father, that where two or more are gathered, You are there. Thank You for Your presence in my life. May I return my pain to You and trust You with all of it today.

You are the Great Healer.

May I find unity with other believers in You.

Amen.

Questions for Reflection

1. Have you ever been hurt by the church? What steps did you take to deal with that pain, or do you feel it hasn't been dealt with?

2. If you answered that it hasn't been dealt with, what steps could you take to begin the healing process in relation to that pain?

3. Is there a time when you had to walk away from, or take a break from, your church because of struggles you were experiencing?

4. Can you relate to the idea of consumerism in church? Have you ever struggled with a consumer mentality when attending church?

Invitation to Return

One Minute: Take some time to pray for the church leaders, elders, youth pastors, worship leaders, and those who serve the church in any capacity. They are imperfect people just like you and me. Ask God to show you if there is any anger or bitterness you are holding in your heart against those in the church who have hurt you, and confess this before Him. Trust Him with this pain and lay it down at His feet.

One Hour: Friend, do you long for some kind of community or connection? Lift that desire to God. Pray about what steps He wants you to take. It may be joining a Bible study or a mom's-day-out group, or He may want you to serve in some capacity wherever you are planted. Take some time to bring this desire before the Lord in daily prayer. Trust He will lead your next steps toward community, wherever that may be.

One Day: Look back at the result of your prayer time in the last activity. Where did God lead you to find community? Once you have confirmation, find time in your schedule to go where He's called you. Remember, God is with you.

15

RETURN TO SEE, HEAR, AND SERVE

Become His Hands and Feet

Christ has no body now but yours,

No hands, no feet on Earth but yours,

Yours are the eyes with which He looks compassion

on this world.

—Saint Teresa of Avila

At some point, I stopped really noticing the people next to me. I don't know exactly when it happened. Probably slowly. But I stopped seeing the people walking by me, waiting in line with me, and sitting across from me. I was solely focused on my phone.

I became most aware of my obsession when I was participating in the digital detox with my family and my church community. During that device-free time, I also happened to be dealing with a pesky tick bite on my big toe and trace amounts of ehrlichiosis bacteria in my blood. The side effects and the blood draws to ensure they removed all the bacteria had me in and out of doctors' offices regularly.

Not the best time to be screenless, but there I was, in hardback chair after hardback chair, unable to do what I usually did in the waiting room—scroll. Without my phone to distract me,

I looked up and out at those sitting around me. I was an outsider. Everywhere I looked, people were looking down. There wasn't small talk. There wasn't eye contact or awkward smiles being sent across the waiting room to other patients waiting for their name to be called. When I started to look up, I saw bent necks and hunched shoulders. I saw a world around me consumed by their phones. And it wasn't just in the waiting rooms. It was at stoplights and on the bleachers at games. It was waiting in the line at the grocery store and before the movie started in the theater.

I was the only one not looking down, yet I was seeing a reflection of who I had become. I wondered, when did my phone consume me? I had forgotten how to wait. How to do nothing. How to not be entertained. How to have uncomfortable silence. I had forgotten how to look around and see the needs of others.

Don't get me wrong—technology has its benefits, and there are plenty of things I enjoy about the screens I connect with every day. But instead of living with intentionality, engaged with the community around me, I had chosen to live a life of isolated disconnect. A life of hunched shoulders lost in glowing rectangles. A life where I forgot my soul's need for connection.

I had been fed by the algorithm instead of God and forgot there was a big, giant world of people longing to look me in the eye, desiring just a moment of my time, wanting for me to be fully engaged. I had forgotten to look people in the eye and answer their questions. Forgotten there were people whose hearts were breaking. People whose worlds were crumbling. People who were marginalized. The outcast. The orphan. The widow. The person down the street who just lost her spouse. The friend who was now unemployed.

So many needs. So much heartache. So many upended lives that may be completely transformed by an unexpected act of service performed for no other reason than to say with my hands and feet, "You matter. You are worth it."

Jesus calls us to love and serve one another, and one of the best ways we can love and serve our sisters and brothers is simply to see them as Jesus sees them. To hear them. To get to really know them. And to meet them where they are, with whatever their current needs may be. This is how we become the hands and feet of Christ. Not with our own agendas, but by asking Him to open our eyes to what is before us and to show us where we can meet Him to help with the work He is already doing.

Because He is always working. All around us. Every day. And He is waiting for us to put down our phones and look up and out at a world in desperate need of a savior. A world in desperate need of us to do His holy work as His hands and feet.

Three weeks before our daughter Nylah was born, we found ourselves with our home sold and no home yet to move into. We had put an offer on a short sale and one on a foreclosure, but the banks were moving slowly. The people who had bought our home weren't able to extend their time of move-in. We were about to give birth to our third child, with a three-year-old and twenty-month-old demanding much of our attention and energy. We were homeless and scared.

On the day we had to be out of the house we had sold, our friends, the Quandees, were leaving for a weeklong vacation. They graciously offered to let us stay in their home. People made us meals. My sister drove in from Chicago. And then, the day before the Quandees were coming home, our prayers were answered. We found out we could buy the foreclosed house and close the next day.

For the weeks leading up to our move and the weeks after we closed, we were constantly loved on by our community. My sister painted the girls' rooms in our new home with my husband.

Our house church helped us pack our belongings into boxes and bins. More meals were made. More childcare provided.

The hands and feet of Christ were everywhere I turned. I felt seen. I felt heard. With every act of service performed, I felt the love of the Lord pierce my soul in new and profound ways.

I was served, and I longed to serve.

I was being seen, and I longed to see.

The ripples of each pebble of service tossed our way stretched far and wide. As my eyes were opened to those around us who were loving us so well, I realized this life of seeing and service and community is what we've been called to.

We are called to serve not just those we know, but also those we do not know. The person sitting next to us in the waiting room with the tear slipping down her cheek. The elderly woman struggling to carry her grocery bags to her car. The mom at the point of breaking as she watches her toddler melt down in the Target checkout line. Our service extends to them, too.

We are all in this broken world together. We all find ourselves in need of a hand. Sometimes, the hand is extended to us. And sometimes, we are the ones with hands extending.

Return to Jesus

Growing up Catholic, I learned to recite many prayers by memory. One of the first prayers I remember learning is the Lord's Prayer. As a young child, I didn't really understand the significance of these words—the way the Lord instructs us to pray. Now, my heart relishes this sacred example Jesus gave us of how to interact intimately and intentionally with our Father above.

This, then, is how you should pray:

> Our Father in heaven,
> hallowed be your name,

> your kingdom come,
> your will be done,
> on earth as it is in heaven.
> Give us today our daily bread.
> And forgive us our debts,
> as we also have forgiven our debtors.
> And lead us not into temptation,
> but deliver us from the evil one.[1]

In this rich prayer from the Son's lips to the Father's ears, Jesus reminds us of what is important: the heart of God. He points our eyes to the Father in heaven and asks that we acknowledge His power and holiness. Then Jesus tells us to ask for God's kingdom to come to Earth. That His will be done here as it is there. Now. In this moment.

Read carefully, friend: Jesus just dropped a bombshell. We do not have to wait until our final breath to experience God's kingdom. We can experience this kingdom of angels singing and praising, of arms lifted and extended, while our feet touch the grass. We can know this holy domain as our eyes lock with the stranger sitting on the bleachers next to us at the T-ball game.

We ask for God's will to be done. "What is Your will, Father?" Then we look, we listen, and we respond. We make this life on Earth not just about us anymore; we make it about Him. About connecting with the Father, hearing His voice, and moving when He says "move." We make our short lives in this world about serving God, about becoming His hands and feet as we live in community with one another.

And when we open our eyes to this kingdom of heaven extended down to Earth and ask the Lord to show us His will, we are living counterculturally. We are inviting His kingdom to come. Now. In this moment.

I was blessed to live in a countercultural moment of love and service. I witnessed true community built on tragedy, service, and a deep, all-encompassing love of the Lord. I saw the hands and feet of Jesus here, on Earth.

While R. D. was recovering in the hospital and Emily was transitioning to life post–bone marrow transplant, I had no choice but to put down my phone. I couldn't avoid what was in front of me every day. I had to face the reality of shattered and broken lives for so many. I had to engage in the healing. The only way to move forward from such heartache was to not only turn to the Lord but also to jump headfirst into community, and I saw love in action.

Our church renovated Jill and R. D.'s home to make it wheelchair-accessible. People made meals for their family and for ours while we cared for Kylie. Emily had moved from the hospital into a short-term living apartment in Indianapolis, but her husband worked hours away in Fort Wayne, so friends and family would take turns staying with Emily in her apartment. My friends from church signed up to bring Emily meals regularly. They decorated her apartment for Christmas, purchased gifts for her young boys, and, when Emily returned to the hospital for a few nights due to complications, they sang Christmas carols on her floor. Many of my friends had never met Emily, but that didn't matter. They knew her story and wanted to help.

All around me, every day, I saw people show up in ways I could not fathom. And my heart was more overwhelmed by these acts of service than by the pain that was propelling them. The kingdom of God had arrived on Earth, and I was a witness to the beauty of it all.

When I look back on this time, I realize that the struggles we all were facing inspired us to constantly turn our gaze to the Lord. We could not do it on our own. The suffering was too great. As we communed with Jesus, we attuned our hearts to his. We looked up and around and saw the world with His eyes.

A father who would never walk again. A husband with three small boys coming to grips with the fact that he may lose his wife to this disease. A mother writing goodbye letters to her boys. Young children faced with the cruelness of the world at a time when most parents are trying desperately to preserve their children's innocence and protect them from this reality. Mothers and fathers looking at their adult children whose lives should just be starting but are now envisioning a new future—one they never could have imagined. And all of us realizing we are help-less to fix these things. All of us crying out to the Lord.

We returned to Jesus for His guidance. His mercy. His help. His relief. His healing. The more we returned to Him, the more our gazes shifted from inward to those around us. The more our hearts were propelled to serve as Jesus's hands and feet to those in need. We weren't living a life of independence anymore. We were living a life of community, with God at the center of it all. We were living counterculturally.

While pain motivated our countercultural living, that time in my life still stands out as one of the most heart-wrenchingly beautiful. I learned to look up and out. I learned what true com-munity means. I learned to abide in His grace and His love. I learned to trust Him with those things that are filled with heart-ache and watch as He meets the very real needs of His people.

When I get lost in the busyness of my days or the scroll of my phone, I think back to that time when I learned what it really means to be the hands and feet of Jesus. I remember God's peo-ple showing up when it wasn't convenient, when it wasn't easy, when it didn't fit nicely into their schedules, because the call from the Lord superseded all. And then I remember the invita-tion to shift my gaze to Jesus. An invitation to look up and see people through His eyes. An invitation to respond to the hurt in the world by spreading kindness and goodness through action. So I willingly put my phone down, turn to my neighbor, and say hello.

More of Jesus.

Less of me.

Be His Hands and Feet

God is calling you to minister to the people around you. Not sure where to start? Your ministry is your *now*—wherever you are, whatever you are doing. Even in this moment, where you are sitting right now—the office, the kitchen, the bathroom (no judgment, God works on social media, too)—and wherever you may be called to go in this day—the grocery store, the dentist, the movies—this is where your ministry resides.

But it's so hard to hear from the Lord when we're so distracted. We can't see where God is working when we are looking down. We can't hear His whispers calling out when the noise from our phones screams louder. We cannot serve others when we aren't even aware that we've stopped looking at them.

Are you spending your time watching Reels while waiting for your food at Taco Bell? Are you looking down at the latest news while you stand in line at the DMV? Are you listening to a podcast while exercising at the gym? Are you checking Yelp reviews while you stand outside of the elementary school, waiting for your child to be dismissed? Did you just pick up your phone to check your texts or even the time?

I have been there more times than I can count. I have missed out on so many opportunities to serve because I have wasted precious moments hunched. I have missed time spent with my family, ministering to them, and truly seeing them standing or sitting right before me. My children have begged for my attention, and I've replied "just a minute" because I had to finish looking down before I could look up to see their artwork, or their smile, or the new trick they just learned. I have missed connecting with strangers who needed a loving hand or with people in my community who have tangible needs I could help fill because I have been lost in the glow of the rectangle.

When you come to the end of your life, it is the connections you made with others that you will remember. That is what you will hold dear. You probably won't remember the TikTok video or the cat meme or the comment on the thread or what Susie had for dinner last Tuesday. But you will remember the times you looked up and out into the eyes of those you cherish, and the sacred moments spent with them. You will remember the way it felt to smile at a stranger and to offer a hand to someone in need. You will remember how it felt to be standing in the presence of the Lord, hear His call to love, and care for those in your community.

Your memories will lie with the aging neighbor you met with every week to bring bread and company. They will rest on the children who gathered around your table for Bible studies and the families that crowded into your living room for small groups. They will lie with the neighbors you enjoyed a glass of wine with after a long day and the connections you made at the monthly book club. You will remember the mom at Target and the word of encouragement you gave when she needed it most. Your heart will rest on the stranger you saw crying at church and the tissue you offered. You will smile when you think of the homeless man and the warm jacket you gave him on a cold winter's eve.

You won't remember what someone's social feed contained, but you will remember the ways you lived intentionally and counterculturally, being the hands and feet of Jesus. You will remember those you loved in a moment of Christ-led service and those who loved you the same. You will remember the times you chose to fully live, eyes wide open, in a world that begs you to be distracted and independent with eyes turned in.

So let's make putting down our devices a priority. Try it for a month. See what happens.

When you are in the waiting room—look up and see.

When you are sitting on the bleachers—look up and see.

When you are at the stoplight—look up and see.

When you are sitting at the restaurant—look up and see.

When you are at the table with your loved ones and in the walls of your home—look up and see.

Don't be afraid to be bored. Don't be scared to think. Don't worry about what will happen if you truly feel those feelings you've been pushing down and the dam of emotions breaks and spills forth.

Put down your phone. Open your eyes to what is happening around you. As you intentionally live in the present and see the people around you, God may whisper in your ear, "They need Me, and I need you to help them."

You may feel His Spirit moving you to act. To say a prayer for them. To ask them how you can help today. To offer them a meal. To pay their check. To compliment their hair. To tell them how good they are with their children.

These acts and words of service may feel funny at first. You may not be used to loving someone in action for the sake of love itself. You may not feel comfortable approaching a stranger to say "Can I help you carry that?" or "Can I pray with you?" Stepping outside of the world we've been taught to reside in can feel odd—uncomfortable, even. But the more you return to Jesus, the easier living a life looking for others to serve will become. And once you start living with head up, eyes open, ears hearing, feet intentionally stepping, you will experience a profound depth and soul quenching unparallel to any other.

So lift your head. Look around. Feel the warmth of the sun

and the coolness of the gentle breeze. Hear the children talking. Smell the fresh flowers blooming in the springtime sun. Make eye contact with your neighbor driving by, and wave as you greet one another. Say hello to the stranger walking her dog on the trail.

Listen for the whispers of the Lord. Hear His voice. Move to the rhythm of His Spirit. Fill the need. Be His hands. Be His feet.

This is the life you were made to live.

This is the life your soul longs for.

Rhythms of Return

Prayer

One Who Sees,

I live distracted, preoccupied, self-absorbed, and unaware of Your voice in my ear, but I long to be present in Your presence.

Help me to make space in my days. To hear Your call. To see with Your eyes. To put down the glowing rectangle full of other people living, and instead to really live the gift of my life to the full.

Open my eyes to where You are working.

Open my ears to Your whispers.

Help me to make space for You as I set down the device and learn to see what's happening in my present. In this ministry You have called me to.

May I go forth and love well.

Today and always.

Amen.

Questions for Reflection

1. When was the last time you picked up your phone? Do you feel your device keeps you from interacting with people around you throughout the day? What about when you're not at home? How often do you look at your phone instead of talking to people

around you—in the school pickup line, at the dog park, in a restaurant?

2. Has there been a time in your life when you have experienced God's kingdom on Earth through the actions of others? What stands out to you about this time?

3. If you answered yes, what did you learn during this time? Did you feel more connected to the Lord and those around you?

4. What does it mean to you to be the hands and feet of Christ?

5. Has there been a time when others have been the hands and feet of Christ to you in your life? What was the impact of their love in action?

Invitation to Return

One Minute: Pause. Look up. Look around. What do you see? What do you hear? What do you smell? What are you feeling? Let your thoughts rest on the presence of God. Ask Him to whisper something in your ear. Ask Him if you can be His hands and feet today. Be present in the now.

One Hour: Ask the Lord where He would have you serve. Is this something like volunteering for a local organization? Or making meals for people who you know are in need and dropping them off on their doorsteps? Or offering free babysitting to a couple with young ones for the day? Trust that God will show you the way, then journal His responses.

One Day: Mark a day off on your calendar and commit to a full day of service. You can do this by yourself or with a church group, friends, or family.

CONCLUSION

God's timing is always perfect, and it's no coincidence that I am typing these words in this season of my life. In the next weeks, our oldest will graduate from high school, our third will graduate from middle school, and our youngest—the forever baby of the family—will attend his fifth-grade promotion ceremony. We are in a season of transition and busyness in our home. We are stretched thin and worn tired, yet these words I have shared with you have been a regular reminder for me of what my heart, soul, mind, and body need—Jesus.

As I have typed, He has reminded me to return to Him, bask in His presence, and receive all the gifts He longed to give me: Love. Peace. Joy. Certainty. Grace. Reconciliation. Friendship. Wisdom. Discernment. Deep connection. Healing. Unity. And more.

I am reminded of Christmas morning—all the joy my children and my husband and I experience as the kids come down the stairs and are greeted by stockings hanging full on the mantle and presents spilling out from under the evergreen tree weighed down by handmade ornaments from years past. And the reason—*the reason we are doing it all.*

But what if, this Christmas, we all walked down the stairs and ignored what was there? What if we went about our morning as usual, completely blind to all those gifts and all that joy waiting for us—right before our eyes? Wouldn't that be odd? Wouldn't that seem so silly? So painfully, obviously ridiculous? What if, days later, someone walked into our home to find all those presents untouched? They would probably think something was wrong with us.

Who would let those gifts go unacknowledged and unopened? Wouldn't that be preposterous?

But what I am realizing is that every day, I so often brush past the gifts waiting for me as I press forward in my hurried state. My to-do lists and spiritual boxes vying for my attention. My need for a productive, "good Christian" lifestyle at the forefront of my mind instead of my need to sit at the feet of Jesus and rest in His presence. I'm invited to a warm blanket of His love and grace, but I press on and don't even pause to acknowledge the invitation and receive the gift that will transform my days, my weeks, my years, and my life.

But I am learning. As I have met with the Lord and have thought of my own habits, practices, and rhythms of return, I have found my life transformed. I have found my heart renewed. I have found a peace that has settled in my spirit, even when chaos swirls around me. I have found joy that has welled up from the depths and burst forth in the most unlikely of times. I have found anxiety quieted and found healing for things I did not know I needed healed. I have found there are so many more ways to find Jesus and meet with Him and see Him and abide in Him and rest with Him. I have found a longing and a hunger that grows the more and more I sit in His presence.

Because that is what He does.

Jesus transforms. Jesus renews. Jesus heals.

He is the Grace-Giver. The Peacekeeper. The Miracle Worker. The Provider. The Comforter. The Joy-Filler. The Unity-Maker.

The Storm-Calmer. The Healer. The Way. The Truth. The Life. Our ever-present help in times of trouble.

He is Love. Love that we cannot begin to comprehend with our limited human understanding. Love that has created all and flows through all and is available for all to take hold of. Love that wants to invade our hearts and be the anchor we hold on to above all else. Love that wants to be shared. Love that excludes nobody and is available for all.

Jesus is waiting for us to give it all to Him. To stop and acknowledge Him. To sit with Him. To understand that our return doesn't have to happen a certain way but can happen in whatever ways fit us best in whatever valleys and mountains and in-between roads we find ourselves in.

He is with us. He is Love.

And Love is inviting us to return.

ACKNOWLEDGMENTS

How do you say thank you to all those who have touched your life and your heart? There is not enough space. There are not enough pages. But I will do my best with the space I have been given. This is my attempt to honor you, my loved ones, but please know, there are not adequate words to express the depth of gratitude I have for you and the places you each hold in my heart.

To my mom: I have always felt loved deep and true by you. Thank you for the sacrifices. For teaching me what it means to be resilient. You are a constant in my life—like the sun that rises and sets. Thank you for always encouraging me to follow my dreams.

To my dad: I have known for as long as I have known the sky is blue and the grass is green that I can come to you with anything and you will not judge. You have modeled unconditional love and have taught me how to laugh, dance, and cry openly, regardless of who is around, and that true friends are worth pursuing.

To my stepdad, who I also call Dad: thank you for loving me as your own and never giving up on me. You have always shown up. Now, you do the same with your grandchildren. Thank you for showing the power of love displayed in action.

To my stepmom, who I affectionately call NanaAOmom: you

have taught me that you can be brave and pursue healing at any point in life. Your love of books and plants, your faith, and your witty sense of humor have shaped so much of what I love and who I am today.

To my stepmom, Carol: you embrace the YOLO mentality, and it is contagious. Thank you for our conversations, your honesty, and all the ways you inspire me.

To my sisters, Lynda and Sarah, and to my brother, Andrew: thank you for the laughter, tears, support, late-night talks, honesty, love, and fun we share. I know I can go to you with anything. To my brothers-in-law, John and Taylor: you are not family by blood, but you may as well be. You add so much simply by being you.

To my nieces, nephews, aunts, uncles, cousins, and the grandparents who have gone before me: you have helped to shape and mold me with your wisdom, faith, life lessons, sacrificial love, and examples.

To my in-laws—Shirley, Sarah, Jeff, Greg, Chris, and their spouses—my bonus family by marriage: thank you for your acceptance and the love you have shared over the years.

To Cindy, with thoughts of Bill in heaven: thank you for modeling a life of faith. Thank you for praying and not giving up on me.

To my mentor, Ro Elliot: thank you for the times when we study the Bible or the Enneagram or just share life with one another. Thank you for helping me to heal, for the wisdom you share, and for the love you give freely.

To my pastors and those who have guided my spiritual walk and growth: thank you for speaking truth and for encouraging me to live in the love of Christ.

To Gardner Literary and my agent, Kristy Cambron, who believed in my writing and gave me a chance: I would not be where

I am today if it weren't for your faith in me and my words. I love working with you and consider myself blessed to have you as not only my agent, but also my friend.

To WaterBrook and my editor, Kimberly Von Fange: thank you for believing in this book. I appreciate all the time, effort, and energy you have poured into making this dream of mine a reality.

To Leslie Means and the Her View from Home team: thank you for sharing my words and for putting my stories in your books. You have helped to make my dreams come true.

To my beautiful writer friends: thank you for your support, the words you have shared, and the prayers you have prayed. Melissa, Amy, Mikala, Jenny, Kelsey, Kelli, Jennifer, Elizabeth, Lisa, Jillian, Emily, Danielle, Mehr, Christine, Angela, Cassie, Tasha, Sarah, Courtney, Whitney—the list is long and wide. You inspire me daily.

To those I have gathered with over the years to study the Word and to talk about the real of life: I would not be where I am if it weren't for you. Gathering with you in basements, in living rooms, around kitchen tables, and in all the other spaces we have met to pray, study, heal, and grow have been some of my deepest points of spiritual growth and connection. You know who you are, and there aren't enough thank-yous.

To the middle school and high school tweens and teens who have gathered around my table with me and my children to study the Word and talk about friendship, faith, and the struggles of growing up—Maizy, Natalie, Maddy, Olivia, Kristyn, Emma, Annaross, Katie, Izzie, Izzy, Izzy (yep—three of them), Aubrie, Hudson, Eli, and Noah. You have taught me more than I have taught you. Of this I am certain.

To my girlfriends (and again to my siblings who are also my best friends, too): I cannot imagine my life without you. Our coffee dates. Walks. Meals shared. The kitchen dance parties. The ways we have helped and supported one another over the years. There is not enough space in a collection of books to give you the recognition you deserve for the tears, laughter and growing up that we've done together. You have helped me with my children. You have gone with me to my darkest places. You have hugged me in times of sorrow. You have laughed with me until we have cried. Jenn, Kristen, Beckie, Beth, Jill, Lisa, Charlotte, Vanessa, Angie, Colleen, Katie, Carrie, Kristy, April, Carrie B., Tanya, Chel, Amber, Tara, Mari, Rebecca, Jennifer, Carrie C., Audi, Sarah, Mikaela, my dear Emily in heaven . . . the list goes on and on. I would name every one of you if I could. You are my people. You know who you are. And I love you.

To the families who have become family to us—the Sproulls, Stantons, McCools, Kelleys, Sheas, Ramos and Baratto, Boyds, Kneppers, Wetzels, Applegates, and Grotes: thank you for loving my family as your own.

To Jenn Sproull: thank you for always being there and taking the time to read through each of these chapters as I was first writing this book. Knowing I can go to you with anything brings my heart comfort.

To my children: Sophia, thank you for your sense of humor, creativity, willingness to try new things, and sense of adventure. Amelia, thank you for your joy, empathy, compassion, and loving spirit. Nylah, thank you for your strong will, determination, individuality, and passion. Patrick, thank you for your fun spirit, infectious laugh, kindness, and the gentleness you share. You all make my world better and my days brighter. One of my greatest joys in life is being your mom.

To Patrick, the love of my life, my soul mate: You are the yin to my yang. Your faith, provision, kindness, gentleness, humor, and dedication to all you put your mind to do not go unnoticed.

Thank you for believing in me when I did not believe in myself and for all the ways you have supported my dreams. I could not have done any of it without you. I love you.

And to you, my reader: thank you for picking up this book. Thank you for going on this journey with me. My heart is eternally grateful, and my prayers go forward with you as you return to Jesus in all your days.

NOTES

Chapter 1: Return to Love

1. John 3:16
2. John 15:13
3. John 15:13, NLT
4. 1 John 4:19
5. John 19:30
6. Ephesians 2:4–5

Chapter 2: Return to Peace

1. John 14:27
2. Matthew 11:28
3. 1 Thessalonians 5:17, NLT

Chapter 3: Return to Comfort

1. Matthew 27:46
2. John 20:25–27
3. Luke 22:17–19
4. John 11:23–26
5. John 11:35
6. Matthew 26:21
7. John 11:3
8. John 11:4–7
9. John 11:32
10. John 11:33
11. "1145. dakruó," Bible Hub, biblehub.com/greek/1145 .htm.

12.   John 11:41–44

13.   *Night of the Living Dead,* directed by George A. Romero (1968, The Criterion Collection).

14.   Matthew 14:13–21

15.   Matthew 15:29–39

16.   John 14:16, KJV

Chapter 4: Return to Grace

1.   *Back to the Future,* directed by Robert Zemeckis (1985, Universal Pictures).

2.   Ephesians 1:7

Chapter 5: Return to Restoration

1.   Matthew 22:34–40

2.   1 Peter 2:9, ESV

3.   Psalm 139:13–16, ESV

4.   1 Corinthians 3:16, ESV

5.   1 John 4:9

6.   2 Corinthians 5:17, ESV

7.   1 Peter 2:24, ESV

8.   Ephesians 1:7, ESV

9.   2 Corinthians 5:20, ESV

10.   James 2:23

11.   Matthew 5:1–12

12.   Matthew 5:13

13.   Matthew 5:14

Chapter 6: Return to Connection

1.   Proverbs 22:6, NKJV

2.   Matthew 18:20

3.   Mark 14:17–18

4.   Mark 14:22–25, NLT

Chapter 7: Return to Repair

1.   "Via Dolorosa," Tourist Israel, touristisrael.com/via -dolorosa/28670.

2.   Luke 23:34
3.   Romans 6:23
4.   2 Corinthians 5:21
5.   Matthew 7:3–5

Chapter 8: Return to Wisdom

1.   *The Chosen,* directed by Dallas Jenkins, written by Dallas Jenkins, Ryan Swanson, and Tyler Thompson (2017–2024, Angel Studios).
2.   Menachem Posner, "Shabbat Shalom," Chabad.org, chabad.org/library/article_cdo/aid/2313062/jewish/Shabbat-Shalom.htm.
3.   Exodus 20:8–11
4.   Mark 3:1–5
5.   Mark 6:31–32
6.   Lysa TerKeurst, *The Best Yes* (Thomas Nelson, 2014), 68.

Chapter 10: Return to Kindness and Gentleness

1.   1 Corinthians 13:4–8
2.   Lysa TerKeurst, *Good Boundaries and Goodbyes* (Thomas Nelson, 2022), 183.

Chapter 11: Return to Unity

1.   John 13:34–35, MSG
2.   1 John 1:7
3.   Romans 3:22
4.   Ephesians 4:2–6
5.   1 Corinthians 12:12–27
6.   2 Corinthians 6:16

Chapter 12: Return to a Life Free from Judgment

1.   Luke 18:42
2.   John 9:6–7
3.   Luke 5:14
4.   Mark 5:19

5.   Matthew 15:1–12
6.   Matthew 12:1–14; Luke 6:1–11
7.   Luke 5:29–32
8.   Matthew 9:32–34
9.   Matthew 15:6–9, we

Chapter 13: Return to Freedom

1.   Psalm 51:7; Isaiah 1:18
2.   Luke 4:18–19
3.   Psalm 140:12
4.   Luke 19:1–10
5.   Mark 12:41–44
6.   James 1:27
7.   Galatians 3:28
8.   Mark 2:15–17
9.   2 Timothy 1:7
10.   Isaiah 61:1
11.   Romans 8:26–27

Chapter 14: Return for Healing and Guidance

1.   Luke 8:43
2.   Luke 8:44–47
3.   Luke 8:48
4.   Proverbs 27:17

Chapter 15: Return to See, Hear, and Serve

1.   Matthew 6:9–13

ABOUT THE AUTHOR

JEN THOMPSON is a blogger, speaker, and author with a heart for sharing the raw and vulnerable pieces of life on her Truly Yours, Jen socials and website. Her comforting and hopeful words are like a warm letter for the soul so you know you are never alone. You can find more of Jen's stories in *So God Made a Mother* and *So God Made a Grandma*.

Jen has a deep love for Jesus and the people He has placed in her life. You can often find her sitting across from a friend at a coffee shop, running around the trails behind her neighborhood, serving the theater kids at the middle and high schools, leading Bible studies for tweens and teens around her kitchen table, driving kids from here to there in her blue minivan, or lying on the couch next to her family with peanut butter surprise in hand.

For the past eighteen years, Jen Thompson has been a stay-at-home mom to her beautiful children: Sophia, Amelia, Nylah, and Patrick. She is married to the love of her life, Patrick, and resides in Nolensville, Tennessee, with her beloved family and two Persian cats—Zilly and Beans—who rule the house.

trulyyoursjen.com

ABOUT THE TYPE

This book was set in Berkeley, a typeface designed by Tony Stan (1917–88) in the early 1980s. It was inspired by, and is a variation on, University of California Old Style, created in the late 1930s by Frederic William Goudy (1865–1947) for the exclusive use of the University of California at Berkeley. The present face, in fact, bears influences of a number of Goudy's fonts, including Kennerley, Goudy Old Style, and Deepdene. Berkeley is notable for both its legibility and its lightness.